FAMILY PROBLEMS
    AND WHAT TO DO ABOUT THEM

BOOKS BY WALLACE DENTON
Published by The Westminster Press

*Family Problems
  and What to Do About Them*

The Minister's Wife as a Counselor

What's Happening to Our Families?

The Role of the Minister's Wife

FAMILY PROBLEMS AND WHAT TO DO ABOUT THEM

By

WALLACE DENTON

THE WESTMINSTER PRESS

Philadelphia

ISBN 0-664-24908-6

Library of Congress Catalog Card No. 71-139690

BOOK DESIGN BY
DOROTHY ALDEN SMITH

Published by The Westminster Press ®
Philadelphia, Pennsylvania

PRINTED IN THE UNITED STATES OF AMERICA

To
WAYNE E. OATES

CONTENTS

INTRODUCTION

This book is written for, and about, you—an ordinary family. It concerns the "man on the street." It is for ordinary husbands and ordinary wives—who naturally have extraordinary children! Most of us are ordinary people. We worry about our children, fuss about the boss, stew over getting the house cleaned, feel guilty over yelling at the kids, look forward to the weekends, wonder what we will have for supper, wait for the next paycheck, watch television at night, think about our religious faith, and sometimes wonder why the relationship between us and our mate has lost some of its sparkle.

Ordinary. It's a good word! Among other things, the word suggests that we all stand equal—no better, no worse than the next guy. But it does not mean that we are all the same! Each family has its own uniqueness, its own style of life, its own distinctive approach to living together. And that, too, is good. The intent of this book is not to make us all alike.

Because we are not all alike, not everything in this book will "speak to your condition." Because we do not all think alike, you will not agree with everything herein. You are not expected to. The author makes no claim of having received these pages on graven tablets of stone. The subjects herein do deal with some of the problems the writer as a marriage counselor has confronted time and again while working with troubled families. Whether you agree or disagree, he hopes your thinking will be stimulated, some new light shed on your situation, and perhaps some suggestion made for dealing more creatively with the everyday problems of *your* ordinary family.

The experiences of the husbands and wives cited herein are real, though names have been changed and the material has often been disguised for their protection. Much of what I know about families has been taught to me by those who have opened up to share with me some of the deep-moving concerns of their lives. To these, my teachers, I am indebted.

I am also indebted to Mrs. Kathleen Fritts, one of those rare persons who not only is a master typist but also is able to decipher my cryptic instructions on a badly marked up manuscript.

As always, I am indebted to my family. Three previous books have not discouraged my wife, Juanita, from once again serving as an "editorial assistant." And Wayne and Susan, who have been cheated out of their father's time and attention by this book, are now ready to "cash" my promises for long daily afternoon walks together.

W. D.

Chapter 1

ORDINARY FAMILIES
IN THE SEVENTIES

Ordinary families never had it so good. They live well. Yet, families of the '70s are in trouble. Voices from some quarters ask whether the family will survive the chaotic turmoil created by the multitude of changes taking place both within and around families. With the writer of the hymn "Abide with Me," they join to say, "Change and decay in all around I see." Multitudes are worried about rebellious children, violence in the streets, riots on campus, men doing "women's work" and women doing "men's work," premarital sex, extramarital sex, homosexuality, easy divorce, rising illegitimate births, increasing incidence of venereal disease, loss of respect for authority, and pliable moral standards.

This chapter will discuss some of the changes affecting contemporary families and will conclude with a discussion of trends that we might expect in our families in this decade of the '70s.

Families in the '70s: Will They Succeed or Fail?

Whether families succeed or fail in the '70s depends partly on the goals or functions that one perceives as being proper for the present family. The traditional family, yesterday's family, served eight basic functions: production, protection, recreation, education, religious instruction, procreation, socialization of the child, and providing emotional security. Production, in particular, has been taken over by factories and shops outside the home. In farm families of a century ago the home was a beehive of activity with the home producing its own food, clothing, tools, furniture, and shelter. Compared to that home, the modern one is a failure, since little but ice is produced in the present home. The wife does not even have to wash the dishes of a TV dinner!

Look at the other traditional functions. Protection has been taken over by the police, welfare agencies, insurance companies, and courts. Education has been taken over by the schools and colleges. Recreation has been commercialized. Even television in the home brings entertainment from outside the home. Religious functions of the home have, for the most part, been relegated to the church, if they exist at all.

Some developments could even threaten the reproductive function of the home. There are scientists who say that sometime during the next century it will be possible to take a sperm and an egg, fertilize them outside the body, and nurture the growing baby by means of a mechanical womb.

These, and other more current changes within the family, lead some persons to conclude that the days of the family are numbered. However, more thoughtful scholars are not so pessimistic about the future of the family. Talcott Parsons, the best-known and most influential sociologist of our day, sees the conflicts of the present as what we might call sparks off the anvil of adjustment. He sees the family, rather than being in a state of decay, as being more important in some ways than ever before. To be sure, the family is giving up some of its functions to other agencies and institutions. But he says the family is specializing on certain vital functions that it still maintains. Among these vital functions are the socialization of the small child and the meeting of the deep needs of family members for emotional security. (*Family, Socialization and Interaction Process,* pp. 10–11.)

Students of the family are aware that it is a rather durable institution, for it has survived the countless depredations of wars, social upheavals, economic crises, slavery, persecutions, and even the glorification of celibacy as the ideal life. As far as we can see into the future, men and women will continue to seek out each other and establish a relationship within which children will be born and cared for, and within which each will meet some of the deep-moving needs that we as humans have to share profoundly in another's life, to give and receive love.

In the meanwhile, there are many families who are caught up in the whirlpool of our changing times, families who are sucked into the vortex of social crises. Anxiously they seek answers. None of us escapes unscathed by these crises. To a greater or lesser degree they have touched us all for good and ill.

SEARCHING FAMILIES IN THE '70s: DIAGNOSING OUR PROBLEMS

Behavior can be viewed as a person's attempt to find an answer to a problem. When one child strikes another, this is his answer to the problem of, "How do I get my toy back?" When a wife becomes involved in an extramarital affair, her behavior represents her answer to a problem of, "I feel so unfeminine," or, "My marriage is so stale," or even, "I'll show John that two can play this game!"

If we view the behavior of American families as a kind of search for a solution to their problems, what can we surmise about what they are seeking? What is the nature of their problems?

First, there is the *search for marital roles*. With the crumbling of old, clear-cut masculine-feminine roles, there is a search for new understandings of what it means to be masculine and feminine in our times. One of the major sources of conflict observed by marriage counselors is that of role conflicts. That is, the friction in the relationship is generated by a conflict between what a man expects of himself as a man, husband, and father, and what a woman expects of him as a man, husband, and father. And the same conflicts exist for the wife. For example, whose role is it to take the initiative sexually? This was once clearly the husband's role. But some modern husbands like their wives to share the initiative. Yet, some wives simply cannot bring themselves to do this. They often view it as being basically unfeminine. That their husbands would expect it, may even do something negative to their feelings about their husbands as men. Thus there is a conflict between what the husband expects sexually of her as a wife and what she expects of herself as a wife.

Another role conflict that husbands and wives in the '70s are wrestling with is that of the "head of the house" concept. While most husbands and wives still say they believe that the husband should be the head, there is a great deal of conflict over exactly what that means when interpreted in everyday life. What does one do when it is the wife who makes the wisest decisions, who handles money best, and who has the most influence in the family? Does this mean that her husband is not a real man? Some husbands think so.

Ernest Burgess says the changing and shifting roles of husbands and wives began in the United States on the frontier. ("The Companionate Family," in Hyman Rodman, ed., *Marriage, Family and Society: A Reader,* p. 260.) Survival required the help of all family members. There the amenities of proper society "back east" were inappropriate. The delicate, helpless, clinging wife on the frontier was a misfit and a liability. Initiative, independence, and ruggedness became premium qualities in a wife.

Secondly, there is a *search for personal fulfillment.* As the home has declined as a productive center, many wives have felt an increasing need to center their interests and energies outside the home. Many lament this fact as evidence of the decaying home. However, at least two things are at work here. One is that it is difficult for many women to achieve a sense of significance and personal worth within the modern home. There is little sense of fulfillment in opening a loaf of bought bread compared to baking one. There is little fulfillment in buying a dress compared to spinning the yarn, weaving the cloth, and making the dress, as wives of yesteryear did. Consequently, many wives feel that if they are to derive a sense of meaning from life, to achieve a sense of making some important contribution to their family or life in general, then they must look outside the home. Women comprise nearly 40 percent of the labor force, and a sizable percentage of these are working outside the home merely in search of fulfillment.

Of course, what is true of women is also true of men. That is, the assembly line and much of the office work engaged in by men leave little room for a sense of fulfillment. If they achieve it at all, it must be done outside their work.

Another factor at work in the growing concern for personal fulfillment is the fact, as Richard Farson notes, that when one's material needs are met, then one becomes increasingly concerned with meeting needs for personal fulfillment. (*The Future of the Family,* p. 63.) Our very affluence means that it is no longer necessary to be preoccupied with the survival needs of food, clothing, and shelter.

The '70s will witness a growing concern on the part of both men and women for activities that impart a sense of meaning, direction, and personal fulfillment to their lives.

Thirdly, there is a *search for intimacy.* In his book *Love and Conflict: New Patterns in Family Life* Gibson Winter sets forth the thesis that a major function of the family is that of meeting needs for intimacy. Yet, he sees family members as being caught between the need for intimacy, on the one hand, and the fear of it, on the other. The need for intimacy leads us to search for someone with whom we can share the deepest recesses of our being. We need someone to whom we can open up and say, "This is who I am; this is how I feel; this is what I fear." But intimacy also means that we need to have someone else to reciprocate and open up to us with the same kind of emotional honesty, to let us on the inside of where he lives.

Obviously, this kind of relationship is fraught with danger. We dare not risk letting anyone know what it is really like to be us. Basically we fear rejection. "Maybe he wouldn't love me if he really knew what I am like," we think; or, "I'm afraid she wouldn't respect me if she knew of my meanness, my worthlessness." Consequently, there is relatively little deep "soul sharing" in many families. Rather than be what Sidney Jourard calls a "transparent self" in a book by that title, we expend our energies pulling the shades on the windows of our souls lest someone look into our inner being. Or we engage in what Eric Berne calls "games." And, as he says, a game is a way of avoiding intimacy. (*Games People Play,* p. 18.)

At the root of many extramarital affairs is the search for intimacy. An affair does not usually begin with a search for sex. The deepest reasons are found in the feelings that people report about such relationships. These comments run: "I just felt I could be myself with her"; "I could be me with him and not worry about how he would take what I said"; "It is wonderful to find someone who will listen to and understand me." All of these are expressions of persons who have found intimacy, an intimacy that was lacking in their marriage.

Fourthly, there is a *search for sexual fulfillment.* Whatever else Americans are looking for, there can be no question that they *think* it can be found or resolved in sex. Just as modern couples expect more of marriage in terms of emotional satisfactions, even so do they expect more of their sexual relationship. Perhaps this is no more dramatically illustrated than in the expectation that the wife also achieve "sexual satisfaction." This usually means that she also expects to achieve an orgasm. Consequently, marriage counselors regularly deal with situations in which the wife is bothered because either she does not achieve an orgasm or else she feels that she does not achieve one as frequently as she would like. On the other hand, sometimes it is the husband who is worried because she does not achieve one and he may take this to be a reflection on his masculinity.

Not too many decades ago couples had few such concerns. The wife was not expected to enjoy sex. William Hammond, onetime surgeon general of the United States, wrote that "nine-tenths of the time decent women felt not the slightest pleasure in intercourse." And a European gynecologist, Fehling, labeled "sexual desire in the young woman as pathological." (Morton Hunt, *The Natural History of Love,* p. 319.) Contrast that with the modern wife who sought counseling because she felt cheated out of something since she did not achieve an orgasm *every* time.

One of the myths about marriage in our day is that marriages begin and end in the bedroom. It is true that some problems begin and end there, but research on marital conflict indicates that the major conflicts have their genesis and resolution in other areas of the relationship. Every marriage counselor knows of couples who, by some standards, have a rather poor sexual relationship but yet consider themselves to be happily married. On the other hand, he knows of couples who are ideally mated sexually but who are so mismated in other areas that they are divorcing.

The lack of fulfillment in sex is often related to the lack of intimacy in the total relationship. Couples who get involved in extramarital affairs often report that their sexual experience seemed a natural consequence to the intimacy achieved in the relationship. Even otherwise frigid wives are often passionate lovers under these circumstances. This intimacy certainly is not the whole answer, but it is a part of the answer.

Another reason for the lack of fulfillment is that many people expect too much of the sexual relationship. Society is so permeated with sexual stimuli, and they are exaggerated to such proportions, that reality cannot measure up to the fantasy. Marriage manuals (sex manuals in reality) do not help the situation. Most of these would lead us to believe that suave, masterful husbands who know the right things to say, and the proper erotic zones to caress, take their wives in their arms where they are wooed to a peak of passion and then in the inferno of intercourse they reach simultaneous orgasms before falling blissfully to sleep. Reality hardly matches that picture. Husbands are usually not that masterful, nor wives that passionate.

An excellent antidote to the marriage manual picture of wedded sex is an article by Ernest Havemann entitled "What the Marriage Manuals Don't Say" published in the November, 1962, issue of *Reader's Digest*. In this article the author says that many wives have been led into unrealistic expectations regarding sex in marriage, particularly with regard to the importance of orgasm. Most wives, he says, do not feel the need for an orgasm at *every* experience of intercourse. This is not to say they do not enjoy the occasion. However, women are not as genitally oriented as men. Rather, their satisfaction on these occasions comes from feeling close to the husband, and the sense of being a part of an experience that is meaningful to him. (Another pertinent article is David Mace's "How Men Feel About Sex" in the June, 1963, *Reader's Digest*.)

Lastly, there is a *search for continuing vitality in marriage*. Modern husbands and wives expect a great deal of marriage. They want much understanding, deep and romantic love, intellectual companionship, shared goals and values, sexual fulfillment, emotional support, and deep communication. They have all of this during courtship and early marriage. But the research of Blood and Wolfe and others indicates that, with the passing of the years, the glow of this early relationship tends to tarnish and fade. (*Husbands and Wives: The Dynamics of Married Living,* p. 173.) Many modern couples are not willing to continue such a relationship. They expect these peak moments of love to continue. When they do not, they get bored and seek a new relationship.

Student classroom discussions lead me to believe that many young people view their parents' marriages as dull, drab, unexciting, devoid of "action." They want much more for themselves. Of course, it may be that almost any marriage when viewed from the outside appears rather unexciting. In any case, these students expect their marriages to have more vitality than they perceive in their parents' marriages.

Richard Farson believes that modern couples have more companionship, sharing, and emotional interaction in their marriages than previous generations had. Then why aren't they satisfied? He believes that the answer lies in a paradox about improvement: that improvement does not bring satisfaction. Improvement only brings the desire for more improvement and yet further improvement. We are always dissatisfied with yesterday's improvement. Therefore, much of the frustration with marriage, he says, arises from the *improvement* of family life. (*The Future of the Family,* p. 65.)

Whatever the causes, it is apparent that many couples now consider it sufficient grounds for divorce when they feel that the relationship has become humdrum. "Till death do us part" increasingly means "Till excitement doth cease."

If modern husbands and wives are searching for a new role, for personal fulfillment, for sexual fulfillment, for intimacy, and for continuing vitality in marriage, what might we expect to happen to our families in the decade of the '70s? Let us now devote attention to that question.

THE SHAPE OF THE EMERGING FAMILY OF THE '70s

The shape of the American family has changed in every decade of this century. The '70s will witness further changes. However, it should be emphasized that family life will be basically the same as it was in the '60s. Ten years against the backdrop of history is but the flick of an eyelid. The changes that do occur will be mainly a continuation of changes that are already at work. Some changes have been at work for many years, such as the increasing freedom and equality of women. Others are more recent on the American family scene.

Then what might we expect family life to be like in the '70s? For better or worse, like it or not, below are some of the things I think we might expect.

1. There will be a *greater convergence of male-female roles*. That is, there will be less and less distinction between "man's work" and "woman's work." The "unisex" style of clothes popular in some circles reflects a certain rejection of distinctions based on sex. Women are now employed in almost every occupational category. The number of women employed in former "men only" jobs will

increase. I expect that in the '70s family members will think less and less of power relationships. By the turn of the century, we may have dropped the "head of the house" concept entirely. Women will be less and less willing to occupy a subservient role to men. Few marriage ceremonies now include the word "obey." Women will demand, and get, equal pay for equal work. They certainly do not get this as they enter the '70s. This demand for equality will extend into hitherto untouched areas, such as sports and religion. Already we have two or three lady jockeys. The number of women ministers will grow as fewer and fewer young men are attracted to that vocation.

✓ 2. There will be a *growth of the emotional-psychological bases of marriage.* In agrarian societies people are married to a large degree simply because they need each other's services. A woman needs someone to provide a living, and a man needs someone to perform household functions while he works. That is, there is a strong economic basis for marriage. In the rare case where a woman divorces, there are few employment opportunities for her with which to support herself and her children.

While there is still an economic basis to marriage, modern couples marry mainly because the two partners meet each other's emotional-psychological needs.

✓ 3. *Marriage will be increasingly viewed as a terminable contract.* "Till death do us part" once meant just that— until death. Probably few couples really mean that today. Some marriage ceremonies have already deleted those words. While we do not practice polygamy, our form of marrige is sometimes described as "serial monogamy" or "chronological monogamy."

The divorce level in the United States has remained relatively stable during the past decade. There will not likely be much change in the '70s. But there will be increasing discussion of term marriages in which the marriage contract expires at the end of a certain number of years and is renewable at the option of the couple. The discussion of trial marriages is being revived, though we will just mention the term now. But there will be an increasing number of young people who practice a form of trial marriage. That is, the two simply move in with each other and share the same apartment. If things work out, they get married legally. If not, they separate. This is already being done by thousands of couples. By the year 2000, or shortly thereafter, we may have some form of legally approved trial marriage. It could take the form of the two-stage marriage proposed by Margaret Mead. At stage one the couple gets married with all the rights and privileges of marriage, but does not have children. If the relationship does not work out, divorce is easy and simple, with no alimony or other responsibility. If the couple decides to have children, the young people enter the second stage, which is more difficult to terminate. ("Apprenticeship for Marriage: A Startling Proposal," *Redbook,* October, 1963.)

The point here is, we already view marriage as terminable. The '70s and '80s will see an increasing number of people who view it as such, and some states may make it possible to get out of unsatisfactory marriages with little difficulty.

4. There will be an *increase of emotional interdependency within the family*. Husbands, wives, and children will meet more of their emotional needs in and through one another. This emotional interdependency will grow out of the fact that American families have lost and are losing many of their relationships with close relatives, the kind of people who once met many emotional needs. Their

mobility (the average family moves every five years) makes it difficult for them to develop deep personal relationships with others. Also, with more and more people living in apartment buildings, they will probably get to know their neighbors less well than do families in the suburbs. Consequently, family members are being thrown back upon one another for the meeting of their emotional needs. This trend will increase.

Richard Farson envisions the growth of intimacy within the family in the years ahead. While we do not know how much of this will be achieved in the '70s, he believes that husbands and wives of the future will expect and achieve a greater openness, a greater emotional interaction than present couples do. (*The Future of the Family,* p. 57.)

5. There will be *changes in mate selection patterns.* As people from various backgrounds are thrown together with one another, there has always been a tendency for some of these to get married. Consequently, after World War II numbers of American men married Japanese, English, German, French, and Italian women.

In the '70s we can expect an increase of interfaith marriages as Protestants, Catholics, and Jews are thrown together at work, in school, in college. We can also expect that there will be an increase of black-white marriages as racial barriers in the United States are torn down.

During the '70s we may have some refinement of computerized matches. Experiments with this in the '60s have been largely unsuccessful mainly because we do not know that much about which background and personality traits are most conducive to successful marriage. When it becomes possible to match couples accurately by computer, we might even see a slight decline in the divorce rate, since marriage would then be based on something more substantial than the present "glandular" basis of many couples.

6. *Children in the family of the '70s.* A prime function of the home throughout history has been the reproduction of children. This will not change in the century.

In the '70s we will see a rising tide of interest in limiting family size. No longer will the mother with the *most* children at church on Mother's Day get the rose! Instead, we may give roses to women with *none!* ("Stop at Two" pins in the lapel could become popular—the "in" thing.) There will be increasing discussion of the necessity of limiting family size. More federal funds will be spent on family-planning projects. It is possible that the Catholic Church will change its position on birth control during the '70s. During this decade some voices in the United States will begin to call for penalties on those who have too many children. By the turn of the century, there may be places in the world where a "baby license" is required before one can have a child.

Single-parent adoptions (adoption of a child by an unmarried adult) in the '70s will doubtless become much more widely accepted and practiced. Some women in the Women's Liberation Movement are even calling for the right of an unmarried woman to have a baby by artificial insemination.

Richard Farson believes that couples in the future may enjoy their children more. They may come to enjoy them, he says, much as they do consumer products. (*The Future of the Family,* p. 63.)

Because children are spending more years in school, the man on the street can be prepared to spend more money on his children. There is no sign now that colleges will become tuition free, as are the public schools, though this is a possibility before the end of the century.

Perhaps not in the next decade, but before the year 2000, mothers will get some help in keeping up with their children. Electronic transponders will be adapted to be attached to children that will permit the mother at home to track their location on her monitor.

✓ 7. There will be a *continuing clash of changing sex values*. We have no reason to believe that the clash of values—old and new—will diminish much in the next decade. We may find an increase in the incidence of premarital sexual intercourse. Presently, there is evidence that young people's attitudes are more permissive about premarital sexual relations than their behavior. That is, they *talk* a lot more permissive line than they *practice*. (This contributes to an illusion of a sexual revolution taking place.) The generation growing up in the '70s may bring their practice more into line with what they verbalize as permissible. Permissiveness with love will doubtless become the pattern in the decades ahead.

In the '70s parents, churches, and others who believe that sexual intercourse is proper only within the context of marriage will be called upon by their children to do more thinking than they have done thus far on why the children should wait until marriage. The old "trinity of terrors"—conception, infection, detection—has lost much of its weight in the modern world. Effective contraceptives are available, venereal diseases can be treated easily if detected early, and "mobile parlors" (automobiles) and motel rooms minimize the possibility of detection. So why should they wait now? But perhaps conception, infection, and detection were never, to begin with, the most basic reasons for confining sexual intercourse to the context of marriage.

We can also expect to hear voices approving of extramarital sex in the '70s. Already some marriage counselors are saying that there may be circumstances under which this is the best solution to certain problems. This strikes many husbands and wives as inconceivable, but we can expect to hear more approving discussions along that line.

8. *Religion and the family in the '70s.* There will probably be a further decrease in church attendance. There has been a steady decline since 1958 for both Protestants and Catholics. The present young generation, which is largely disinterested in institutionalized religion, will become the adult generation, and children who reach teen years in the '70s will likely continue to hold the same opinion, thus adding to the decline.

Not only will there be a decline in church attendance, but the relative lack of religious influence in the lives of people will doubtless continue. We have little or no evidence that suggests a higher rate of moral behavior among churchgoers than among nonchurchgoers. The peer group seems to exercise greater influence upon a person than does his church.

In the '70s we can expect that religion will become increasingly humanistic. At the same time some envision the growth on the other end of the religious continuum of Pentecostal groups. (*Time,* December 19, 1969, p. 23.) Dr. Roland W. Tapp also predicts that the present "selling point" of the church as a fellowship will become less and less appealing to people who will be guarding more and more their rapidly vanishing privacy. However, it may be that the church will become more meaningful in the future in those instances where genuine koinonia is achieved in small groups within the church.

As the lecture method of teaching declines in popularity, churches in the '70s will turn increasingly to the use of small-group teaching settings. There will be the use of T-group techniques in many churches as ways are sought for making one's religious faith a more vital and dynamic dimension of life.

The author of *The Next 500 Years,* Burnham Beckwith, predicts the eventual demise of religion. Without trying to project five hundred years into the future, suffice it to say that I do not envision such a demise in the decades immediately ahead. Churches will doubtless change radically. But such a prediction fails to recognize a very basic need within man for that which transcends himself—a religious need. Science cannot meet that need.

In this chapter we have tried to look at what families are like as we enter the '70s, what our problems are, what we seek. We have also tried to project ourselves into this decade to see where we are going. Basically family life will remain relatively unchanged. Men and women will still seek out each other and marry after a courtship period. The couple will move into a home, buy furniture, have children, go into debt, quarrel with each other, love each other, enjoy each other, marvel at how their children grow. To be sure, there will be those who depart from this pattern, but they will not be the normative group.

But changes are taking place, changes that are already at work. Some of these excite us. Others frighten us. A few make us want to fight. But the stream of life moves on its inevitable way. Slowly and inexorably, like a vast glacier, it moves ahead sweeping along with it the peoples, families, customs, and problems of the times.

The needs of ordinary families in the '70s will be in the realm of the psychological, the philosophical, the religious, not the material. The observation of Herbert Stroup about families in the last third of this century is pertinent for families in the '70s. Looking into the future, he says: "So, as man faces the future, his major problems are not essentially of a material or technological nature. What he faces are problems involving what it means, individually and socially, to be fully human. He faces the overriding issue of his values. And what we need in the new surge of utopianism is not to be dumbfounded by statistics we hear but to be keen, perceptive, humble, and creative about the *values* we want to have guiding us in the year 2000." (*The Future of the Family,* p. 54.)

Having briefly looked at families of the '70s, we will discuss in the following chapters some of the common problems confronted by husbands and wives of our times.

Chapter 2

THE REAL INTIMACY IN MARRIAGE— COMMUNICATION

It is the end of the day. Alan and Jean have just gone to bed. It has been a busy day; both are tired. Alan has hardly said a word all evening. He is always quiet when tired, but tonight he has been quieter than usual. "You've been awfully silent this evening," Jean observed out of the darkness. "Is there anything wrong?" "Not really," he responded, evading her question. "Guess I'm just tired." Jean wasn't one to give up easily. "Well, it's been a long day, but I thought something special might be bothering you." I can't hide anything from her, Alan thought to himself. Then he decided to level with her. They have always done this with each other.

"Well, this thing at work has been eating on me," he began. "The rumor is out at the plant that they are bringing in these new computerized testers and that our end of the lab might be shut down. If they do, I'm out of a job!" His concern was out now. Then for an hour and a half in the darkness of their bedroom Alan and Jean talked. He poured out his fear of not getting another job; after all, he is forty-six now. He talked of the sense of responsibility that is upon him for the family. He also talked of his resentment of the machines, irrational as it is. Together he and Jean explored what they might do and decided on a plan of action for tomorrow. Then they fell asleep.

It is the end of the same day. Across town another couple, Jim and Kathy, have also just gone to bed. They too are tired but for a different reason. Most of their evening has been spent in a quarrel over the children. It all began when Jim accused Kathy of being a "lousy mother." She in turn accused him of being an "absentee father" and having no interest in the children. The quarrel raged on for more than an hour with charge followed by counter-charge. Finally it stopped. Nothing had been resolved. Instead, it had rather worn itself out, leaving a stony silence in its wake.

Now they are in bed. Jim reached over to touch Kathy in a hesitant peace gesture. She recoiled as if pricked by a pin. He was angered, but persisted. Then he indicated an interest in sex. Kathy, still angry over the evening, accused him of always thinking every problem could be solved in bed. She is less than interested. How could he have said all those things about her only two hours ago, and now be interested in sex? He persisted. Finally she submitted, but not before telling him that he must be some kind of animal, and to hurry and get it over. Eventually they both go to sleep.

Which couple was intimate with each other? Some would say the last couple, Jim and Kathy, were intimate just before going to sleep. Others would say Alan and Jean were intimate as they talked through anxieties concerning his work. Of course, though sexually involved, Jim and Kathy were anything but intimate—even though the word is often used as a euphemism for sexual intercourse. But sexual intercourse does not require intimacy. As with Kathy, it may take place in the context of anger. There was no emotional closeness or sharing. In other cases, a person

may know little or nothing about the sexual partner.

But Alan and Jean were intimate because they communicated (or communed, to use a root word) together.
For, you see, the real intimacy in marriage is not sex.
Rather, it is that sense of openness in which two people
can be themselves, their deeper selves; it is a sense of
being able to "share souls"; it is being able to share one's
deepest hopes, fears, resentments; it is being able to both
give and receive love without reservation. The common
word to describe the sharing of these feelings is communication.

This kind of intimacy is usually achieved during courtship, and it is this sense of being loved, accepted, of feeling safe with the other that is mainly responsible for
propelling us on toward marriage. To be emotionally close
to another without fear of hurt or rejection is a deeply
satisfying experience. This is what young couples expect
to continue in marriage. Too often it fades as quickly as
the honeymoon. With intimacy gone, the couple may simply drift along with the current of time where the days
blend into months, and the months into years, and the
years are numbered by the births of the children, the
houses they have lived in, the jobs he has had. But an
increasing number of couples feel that a marriage in which
intimacy has died is not worth keeping, so they divorce.
Fortunately, other couples work at revitalizing their relationship, to rekindle the flames of intimacy.

Research on marriage regularly reveals the loss of some
intimacy with the passing of the years. Is it too much to
hope that a marriage can be kept alive and dynamic—intimate? No, it is not too much to hope for, but the price
of intimacy is the constant, lifelong task of keeping in

touch with each other, of communication.

Intimacy in marriage is achieved in the ability of a couple to communicate together at deep levels. This is not necessarily the same thing as talking. "Talking" puts too much emphasis on words. "Communication" focuses on the transmission of ideas and *feelings* toward the other. As every sensitive person knows, words can conceal, as well as reveal, one's feelings. These feelings are not all positive; there will be angry ones at times and depressed ones at other times. Talking is not necessarily communication, because we all have known those who can talk all day and never really say anything. Then there are those who can listen all day and never hear anything. Nothing is communicated. This chapter is concerned with keeping intimacy alive in marriage; with the ability of one person to *get through* to the mate, to *communicate*. (As a marriage counselor, I know of many couples who are excellent in *getting at* each other!)

Without this deep communication, intimacy dies. It can be maintained or restored only when both husband and wife are willing to open up to the other—by words, gestures, actions—and let the other know how life looks from his own orientation. But communication is a two-way street. It not only means that we open up to let the other know us, but that we come to understand the other as he in turn opens to us. Without this mutual sharing, marriage becomes a monologue. One of the most interesting phrases in the New Testament is one that Jesus used to describe the prayer of the self-righteous Pharisee who stood in the Temple thanking God he was not a sinner as others. Jesus said the Pharisee "prayed thus *with himself*" (Luke 18:11). His prayer was not communication with God, since he allowed no room to listen to God. It was a monologue. And marriage, like that prayer, can become a mere monologue with each person talking *past* the other rather than *with* the other.

FAMILY CONFLICT AND THE BREAKDOWN OF COMMUNICATION

Marriage and family counselors are often asked by laymen, "Tell me, what is *the main marriage problem* that husbands and wives have?" This is a difficult, if not impossible, question to answer because one does not confront *the main problem*. Rather, a whole complex of problems have contributed to their conflict. However, having said that, if we were to try to dig down to some very basic problems, one of those at the base of much marital conflict is the breakdown of communication between the husband and wife. (Of course, in the first place sometimes there was never any communication to break down.)

Perhaps we could pause here to say that there are those who believe that all problems can be resolved by open communication. They cannot. I occasionally see couples who impress me as doing an excellent job of communicating, but they simply do not want the same things from each other, or they do not share common goals in life. In stating the above, I am also aware that there are some researchers who say we have no evidence that communication and understanding are necessary to a good marriage. (See Richard Udry, *The Social Context of Marriage,* pp. 275–280, for a summary of this research.) Examination of this research reveals, however, that the researchers tend to equate talking with communication, and knowledge of the other with understanding of the other. Both of these are narrow and inadequate definitions of communication and understanding.

The degree of success in marriage is closely related to the ability of a husband and wife to communicate, to understand each other. (Though, as noted above, communication is no guarantee of marital success.) Often I will say to young couples being seen in premarital counseling, "Ten years from now you may not remember much of anything that I've said [the positive approach], but if you do remember anything, I want you to remember this: The degree to which your marriage succeeds or fails will be closely related to your ability to communicate with each other, to understand and be understood." Without communication, intimacy fades, the couple drifts apart, and walls of hurt and misunderstanding build. Sometimes the two feel as if they are no longer on the same team or even playing the same game.

When communication fails and intimacy dies, a couple can quarrel over almost anything—dirty socks on the floor, late meals, or even a gesture. A wife came in for counseling years ago and told of a quarrel she had had with her husband during the week. As she recounted the event, her face flushed and she became angry all over again. Wondering what could have provoked such anger, I eagerly asked, "Tell me, what did he do to make you mad?" With a measured and solemn tone she replied, "He came home from work and walked in the door with *that look* on his face!" That look, but a look is all it takes if a wife already feels alienated from her husband, misunderstood by him, and angry with him.

If a couple can communicate with each other in ways that will make each understand the other, then the two have in their hands the basic tool with which they can repair almost any facet of their relationship, whether this be the children, finances, sex, or other. Without it, they can quarrel violently over the least trivia—even a look on the face.

SOME COMMON BARRIERS TO COMMUNICATION

Why is it that two people who begin marriage with love and intimacy lose their ability to open up to each other with the kind of communication that can sweep away alienating differences? The successful businessman who can deal with the interpersonal problems of a million-dollar business may fail miserably when it comes to ironing out an interpersonal problem with his wife. Of course, the reasons for failures in communication are complex and numerous. At the risk of oversimplifying a very involved matter, let us explore some of the barriers to effective husband-wife communication.

✓ 1. The *fear of being rejected* keeps many couples from communicating with each other. To communicate means that I open myself and let another know what I really think and feel inside. At times I might reveal how angry I am, how much I love, or how deeply hurt I am. But in this act of self-revelation I run the very real risk of being rejected. Suppose the person becomes angry in response to my anger? Maybe he won't want to have anything else to do with me. Or suppose I let him know how much I care about him? He might reject my love, and I will discover that he does not care much about me.

This fear of rejection also shows up in group communication. Have you ever had this happen to you? You are in a group discussion and have a comment to make, but you fear that your observation may be considered superficial or even silly. So you "play it safe" and remain silent. About that time someone breaks in with the very idea you toyed with sharing and the group thinks it is great and spends the next fifteen minutes discussing it. Why did you not open up to share your idea? You feared that the idea (you, really) would be rejected. And the danger of being rejected is enough to keep many silent, and thereby fail to communicate.

2. The *fear of revealing something* that might be used against them also keeps some people from communicating. The life experiences of many have been such that they have learned through numerous painful experiences that if you reveal too much of yourself to another, the person may take advantage of that and later use it against you. After a while these people "get smart" and keep their thoughts and feelings to themselves. In marriage they will also tend to keep their deeper thoughts and feelings to themselves. (Though on the surface, they are often extroverted, happy-go-lucky, and may appear to be open.) For instance, John had always been one to express few of his inner feelings, though his wife, Lil, knew he often felt deeply. Yet, on one occasion in a moment of emotional honesty he confided that sometimes in a quarrel he knew he was wrong, but could not admit so without a loss of face. He has regretted a thousand times ever revealing that to Lil. In nearly every quarrel since then, he says, she has thrown that up to him, clobbering him over the head with it. Perhaps she should not be surprised that he has revealed so little of himself since then.

3. The *fear of being discovered* is a barrier to communication. A fear within nearly all of us is that one's own mate or others will discover that we are not what they

take us to be. They seem to think we are worthwhile. We fear they will discover otherwise if they really get to know us. Men particularly have a problem at the point of being discovered to be weak. They often have an idea that being masculine means they are rugged, independent, self-confident, strong, and don't need anyone. Yet, a fear lurks in the recesses of their minds that if they open up too much, their wives will in fact discover them to be weak. The fear of weakness is the "Achilles' heel" of men. Call a man lazy and he can live with that; call him a poor father and he can live with that; call him a braggart and he can live with that; but don't call him weak! (Remember that "impotence," a basic fear of men, means to be without power —weak.)

Strangely, people have within them two conflicting aspects: the need to be known, and the fear of being known. Every psychiatrist and counselor knows that nestled within the breast of even his sickest patient is a resistance to letting the therapist really know him, even when he knows that getting well depends upon it. In fact, we are even afraid to know ourselves; yet another part of us paradoxically seeks self-knowledge. It is out of this fear of having to face ourselves in the raw that the various defense mechanisms of which Freud spoke arise, mechanisms as rationalization, projection, and denial.

As stated above, one of our needs is the need to be known. One reason people often find an extramarital affair exciting is the refreshing experience of letting someone else come to know them, and the excitement of discovering the other person. Eagerly they reveal certain things about themselves and are filled with a sense of oneness with the other to discover that they too like to do silly little things, as make paper boats with messages written on them and sail them down the river. Couples sometimes report to counselors that they feel bored with marriage because there is nothing new to know or discover about the mate and that they have revealed all of themselves years ago.

4. *Defensiveness* is a barrier to communication. Defensiveness is the tendency to protect oneself unnecessarily from attack. It becomes a barrier to communication because the person is so busy protecting himself that he does not have time to listen to the other. I see this reflected regularly in the behavior of husbands and wives as the one tries to talk and communicate with the other. The one can hardly wait for the other to pause for a breath so as to have the chance to rush in with a defensive "Yes, but . . ." comment in which to proceed to make a defense by giving all the reasons for doing what was done. In doing this, the person misses the meaning in what the other has said. One of the main reasons why a third party can understand what the mate is saying is that, not having lived in the situation, the third person is not emotionally involved and has no need to be defensive and no need to interrupt with "Yes, but . . ."

5. *Differences in family background* may be a barrier to communication. This is often overlooked. It often manifests itself in the decision-making patterns of the home. For instance, here is a girl from a democratic, middle-class background who married a man who had been reared in a home with a patriarchal father from an East European background. Shortly after marriage she was angered and shocked into disbelief when her new husband drove up with an unannounced new family car. In her family, a new car was always a decision to be discussed with the whole family. But, as it came out in counseling, in his family the

patriarchal father always had full and unquestioned charge of the car and did not consider this a matter for discussion with his wife.

Differences in family background may also complicate communication in a couple's affectional life. Although it is not a hard, set rule, there is a tendency for people to express affection as it was expressed in their childhood homes. Consequently, if a man grew up in a demonstrative home filled with many expressions of love and affection, he stands a good chance of both showing and wanting to receive love in the same manner. However, if he is married to a girl who grew up in a home where the family was reserved in such matters, he may be very frustrated by what he interprets as "coldness" on her part and she in turn may feel constantly pulled at for more demonstrations of love and affection.

6. The *lack of time* makes communication difficult. While discussing some of the psychological barriers to communication, a wife in the group said that none of these seemed to apply to her. "Our problem," she continued, "is that we simply do not seem to have time to talk." Then she recounted a day's schedule: They get up, and there is a rush to eat breakfast and get the husband off to work and the kids off to school. No time then to talk. In the evening there is the evening meal. Then she cleans up the kitchen, helps get the homework done, watches a little television, and gets the children ready for bed. By the time the children get up and down a few times and are finally settled in bed, it is becoming rather late and both the husband and the wife are physically and emotionally tired. This is hardly the ideal time and circumstance to deal with any serious matter. She was right, time is a problem! (Counselors always look for deep psychological reasons

behind problems and sometimes overlook obvious ones—such as time.)

GUIDELINES IN LEARNING MORE EFFECTIVE COMMUNICATION

Learning to communicate is no easy matter. Anyone who says otherwise has a superficial understanding of communication. If it were easy, we could give a book on the subject to a couple, they would read it and "live happily ever after." It doesn't work that way. As a matter of fact, there is a whole complex body of knowledge on communication involving semantics, etc. Therefore, as stated earlier, I fear sounding too superficial in trying to offer guidelines on better communication. Nonetheless, if a couple's relationship is not too far deteriorated, perhaps the suggestions to follow may be of help. However, if there is too much pathology, these will be of no help and professional help should be sought.

As the reader will readily note, we are basically concerned here with communication by words, by talking. Obviously, this is not the only way husbands and wives communicate. They also communicate through the written word as well as the spoken word. They, furthermore, communicate by gestures (outstretched arms), facial expressions (a smile), and gifts (flowers). There are other ways in which we communicate something of ourselves to another: in the clothes we wear, the meals prepared, the tastes in interior decoration of the home, etc.

But language is man's most effective mode of communication. Yet, even language is limited. What does a wife mean when she asks her husband, "Where have you been?"

Is it a simple request for information, or is it a reprimand for being late? Only through the use of further language can he know for sure. One of the problems that counselors have in helping husbands and wives to be more effective communicators is that of getting them to put their ideas and feeling into words of plain English. Hints and subtle communications may at times be adequate for couples who are finely "tuned in" to each other, but they are wholly inadequate for couples who are having very much difficulty.

Now, what are some guidelines to better communication?

1. *The place to begin with is the simple (or is it?) decision to try to get through to the mate.* This sounds trite. But couples often feel that they have tried and failed a thousand times, so why try again. They have given up. Consequently, one of their major tasks will be to overcome the inertia that failure has generated in the marriage. However, one mate or the other has to take the initiative for this new effort. Each should not hope for too much response from the other one. It may take weeks of renewed effort before much headway is made in getting through to the other. But without this resolve to try again, the couple is forced to resign themselves to the *status quo,* or at best to live in the hope that somehow, someway, "things will get better." They usually do not.

2. *The timing in approaching the mate is crucial.* There is a best time for trying to talk with the mate. Every person has certain times of the day when he is more likely to listen to another than at other times. There are even certain days when we are more likely to lend a listening ear than others. The time when the husband walks in the front door coming home from work is usually not the best time to hit him in the face with a problem. The time when the wife prepares the evening meal is hardly the best time

to confront her with, "Honey, I must talk with you about our sex life!" The optimum time is not the same for everybody and perhaps not the same for each person every day. Consequently, each person must decide the time that seems most ideal in his situation. For many couples this is right after they go to bed. For others, it is in the morning before they get up to begin the day's routine. In your case, it may be yet another time. Whatever it is, the timing of your approach to the mate will largely determine its outcome.

3. *Some couples find that openly stating the desire to talk helps communication.* It seems that some husbands and wives do not really pay attention when the other simply begins talking of a problem. This is particularly true where the husband or wife has learned to "tune out" the other in order to minimize the anxiety of coping with marital conflict. I have often had a husband and wife together in counseling when, say, the wife tells the husband of her discontent over some facet of their relationship. He seems shocked. I then ask him whether he had known this before and he will say it is news to him. To this she will retort indignantly, "Well, I don't know why it should be, I've told you often enough about it!" Further inquiry may reveal that he has heard her say those words before, but somehow they did not "soak in." As one husband said: "Oh, I didn't know you were really serious. I thought you were just running off at the mouth!"

This problem of thinking that the mate is "running off at the mouth" is minimized in some cases when the husband or the wife openly says, "Honey, when you have time, there is something I want to talk with you about." If the mate has an ounce of curiosity, he or she will want to know what it is that the other wishes to say. In any case, such an announcement will be more difficult to evade than when the mate simply begins talking unannounced.

4. *Readily admit your own shortcomings.* There are some persons who can never admit to being wrong. They always have to be right. But in marriage conflicts, one rarely, or never, deals with guilty and innocent parties. Always each person, to a greater or lesser degree, knowingly or unknowingly, has made his own contribution to the problem.

A husband who begins by saying, "Honey, I know I'm not as sensitive to your needs as I should be, but . . ." is more likely to get a hearing than one who begins immediately as if the wife were the "big bad wolf" and he is the poor, innocent "Red Riding Hood" who has been abused by this vicious and insensitive woman. However, if he does not genuinely mean what he says in admitting his own wrongs, she will sense this as a game he is playing.

5. *Listen with an open ear and a shut mouth.* How difficult this is to do! One of the chief problems in understanding is that we simply do not listen, because we shut our ears and open our mouths. The overpowering temptation is to interrupt and correct the other's misperception of a situation, or to defend our actions. Yet, this is exactly the kind of behavior we detest in others when we ourselves are trying to talk. It makes no difference whether you are dominating as accused by your mate, or whether you are affectionate or not, or whether you have been ignoring your mate or not. What does count is that your mate perceives it this way and has reacted to you as if you are and needs to be able to say so, and you need to hear it said. Only then can you begin to take corrective action.

6. *Listen with your "third ear."* Years ago Theodore Reik wrote *Listening with the Third Ear*. This is an important ear in the act of genuine communication. Often

what is unspoken is more important than what is spoken. The wife may have been fussing about how the husband should stay home tonight, saying that he is too sick to go to the civic club, when the real issue is that she resents him attending the club and feels neglected because of it. But he will never hear that unless he listens with his third ear. (Of course, even she may not be aware of why she does not want him to attend the club.)

7. *Let the mate know when he or she seems to retaliate with personal data revealed "in confidence."* Often a husband or a wife feels that the mate has taken advantage of information revealed almost "in confidence" and is now having it shot back in anger. For instance, Nancy revealed to Bob that she sometimes expressed her anger toward him by promptly going to sleep at night. A few mornings later he commented angrily, "Well, I see you used sex to get at me again last night." Rather than resolve never to reveal anything that personal again, she mentioned this later that day, telling him that she felt he was using it against her. In this case Bob apologized, and they talked about what had happened the evening before.

Often a husband or a wife had no intention of using such information against the other, though the mate thinks this is what happened. If the offended mate says nothing, then the couple is cheated out of a chance to correct the misperception, or otherwise deal with the situation through which their marriage is strengthened.

As noted in this chapter, the act of genuine communication is not easy, nor is it without its dangers. But it can be done. The consequences of failing to communicate are so disastrous that one has no realistic alternative. Without this opening of your soul to your mate and permitting your mate to open his or her soul to you, the sense of relatedness, the sense of intimacy in marriage withers and may die. Few human experiences are so deeply rewarding and personally fulfilling as knowing that with our mate we can safely be our open, unvarnished selves with the full knowledge that because of, and yet in spite of, ourselves, we are still loved and respected. Dinah Maria Mulock Craik (1826–1887) captured this experience of true intimacy and communion in this beautiful passage:

Oh, the comfort, the inexpressible comfort, of feeling safe with a person, having neither to weigh thoughts nor measure words, but pouring them all right out, just as they are, chaff and grain together; certain that a faithful hand will take and sift them, keep that which is worth keeping, and then with the breath of kindness, blow the rest away.

Chapter 3

FIGHT FOR YOUR (MARITAL) LIFE

"Marital quarrels are inevitable," asserted the speaker addressing a gathering of husbands and wives. "If two people live together," he continued, "sooner or later misunderstanding will arise, feelings will be hurt, or some other occasion occur in which tempers will flare and a quarrel ensue." At the conclusion, one wife immediately approached the speaker even before he had left the speaker's stand, and looking him straight in the eye, said, "I want you to know that John and I have been married thirty-five years and we haven't had a disagreement yet!" The speaker made a few noncommittal remarks, but did not disagree with her. Afterward he wondered whether he had not done the same thing John had done for thirty-five years—just not disagree!

The truth of the matter is that a husband and wife *can* live together without disagreements or quarrels—if one does all the thinking! Nearly all husbands and wives quarrel, but many do not care to use the word. Instead, they prefer to say that they have "lively discussions," "noisy differences," "friendly fusses," or some other circumlocution. The words "quarrel" and "fight" seem to strike fear into marital hearts. Perhaps it is assumed that only in unsuccessful marriages do such things happen.

Few, if any, family counselors are favorably impressed by couples who announce (usually with obvious pride), "We never quarrel!" The counselor may, however, be impressed that the relationship can be so anemic without their having discovered it. True, there was a time in which the absence of quarrels was equated with marital success. But in recent years marriage counselors have taken an increasing interest in the constructive aspects of quarrels. We are being forced to face the fact that the inability to cope adequately with anger is at the root of much marital dissatisfaction and dissolution.

It is sometimes assumed that all divorces are preceded by a period of fighting and quarreling. This is not so. Marriage counselors and lawyers regularly work with couples on the verge of divorce, or in divorce proceedings, who say they have seldom quarreled. John and Carol were such a couple. John had always been a quiet, easygoing man. Unknown to his wife, during the fifteen years of their marriage he had intensely resented, among other things, his wife's "addiction" to bridge-playing. As a member of four clubs, she was gone from home four days a week. She also traveled to other states to play in tournaments. As a result, the children spent much time with baby-sitters. John felt that he, the children, and the house were neglected. But because he disliked displays of anger, he said little. Even the occasions when anger did break through, it was so well controlled that Carol was unable to grasp the depth of his resentment. When he announced after she returned from a particular tournament that he was ready for a divorce, she was so shocked that she first assumed he was joking. She thought they were happily married. After all, they never quarreled. However, what she did not know was that for years she had been "hanging" herself with bridge.

As a marriage counselor, I am in full agreement with those who say that we would have fewer divorces in the United States if we had more *good* quarrels! In fact, every couple might very well be issued a plaque for their home at the time of marriage, reading: "Avoid the divorce court: Have a good fight!" John and Carol might very well be married today had they had some good fights. At least she would have had the chance to know how deeply he felt about her bridge-playing, even though this was only a symptom of a larger problem.

On the other hand, each reader likely knows of couples who regularly quarreled and still ended up divorced. An examination of their quarrels will usually reveal that they were aborted or dirty fights. Note that our plaque for the newlyweds reads, "Have a *good* fight." An aborted fight stops before anything is resolved, and dirty fighters engage in unfair tactics such as name-calling and striking at sensitive (but irrelevant) areas.

It is not the purpose of this chapter to try to make fighters out of nonfighting husbands and wives. Perhaps there are those people who ought not to try to engage in a marital quarrel without the aid of a profesional "referee"— such as a marriage counselor. They may have stored up too much anger for too many years to try to get the "lid" off without both partners getting seriously hurt. The leading exponent of marital quarreling today is George Bach, a California psychologist who has a "fight clinic." He too notes that marital quarreling is not for everyone. (*The Intimate Enemy,* pp. 343–344.) However, for those who are already fighters, it is hoped that this chapter can help strengthen their marriages by teaching them how to sharpen their skills in marital quarreling. At the base of this chapter is the belief that from a good quarrel, communication can be established and the marriage relationship thereby enhanced.

THE INEVITABILITY OF MARITAL CONFLICT

Marital conflict is inevitable. This categorical statement will doubtless be disputed by some. Nonetheless, this is the consensus of such specialists in family relations as David Mace, George Bach, and others. Dr. Mace asserts that there will be conflicts, and that "this is true in *all* cases— there are *no* exceptions." ("The Art of Marital Fighting," *McCall's,* October, 1962, p. 50.) Dr. Bach also talks of the inevitability of such conflict and goes on to say that "couples who can't display hostilities are not polite but phony." (*The Intimate Enemy,* p. 36.)

Then if conflict is inevitable, why is there difficulty in admitting or expressing it in a marriage? Part of the answer lies in the image of an ideal marriage that exists in the minds of many. An ideal marriage, these couples believe, involves a conflict-free relationship. Since they have, or like to consider themselves as having, an ideal marriage, they are forced into denying conflict and avoiding quarrels. But in the intimacy of marriage, quarrels can be avoided only by one mate being willing to be completely dominated by the other, by refusing to think, to have opinions and ideas of his own. But note that only *quarrels* are avoided, not *conflicts*. The submissive mate simply swallows conflict or "looks the other way."

There are those who feel that Americans in general have difficulty expressing anger. (Of course, there is good evidence that we also have difficulty expressing love, real love.) Most go out of their way to avoid expressing anger to a colleague at work, a neighbor, a relative, or a friend at church. It is as if expressing the anger would destroy the relationship. This avoidance is not found in all societies. Two women of European origin, but living in New York City, were overheard one day engaged in a wildly heated argument. They appeared to be the deadliest of enemies. Imagine my surprise the next day to see these "enemies" involved in a pleasant and amicable conversation! In their circle, it was perfectly acceptable to be emotionally honest and to express one's anger toward friends, to get it out and over with. But they could also be just as honest and express positive feelings. Two angry American wives would more likely say nothing to each other, and instead fill the ear of the husband or another friend about the incident. In fact, much gossip is nothing more than feeling angry toward person A but expressing it to person B in the form of gossip. Few Americans seem to have learned in a deep emotional sense (though some know it on an intellectual level) that you can be angry with and still love the same person at the same time.

What is being said here is that anger is one of the most basic human emotions. To feel angry is to be human. And we need not apologize for being human—only for being *inhuman*. A person who feels no anger is somewhat emotionally crippled. This person is described by Thomas Fuller as having a "maimed mind." (Cited by D. A. Sugarman, "How to Cool Your Anger," *Seventeen,* April, 1967, p. 251.) I have often noted in my counseling with husbands and wives that those who seem to feel no anger also have difficulty feeling love as well. It is as if the same psychological process of anesthetizing oneself against anger also "deadens" the ability to feel other emotions very deeply.

One of the chief dangers of unexpressed and unresolved anger is that it ultimately succeeds in isolating the husband and the wife from each other. If strong negative feelings toward the mate are suppressed over a period of months or years, they only succeed in building up an accumulation of smoldering, unresolved resentments beneath the surface. This ultimately creates between them what David Mace calls a marital "Berlin wall." This couple should not be surprised that the vital communication and sharing in each other's lives are gradually cut off. They end up at the marriage counselor's office complaining: "We just don't have anything in common anymore. There's nothing to talk about, no place to go, nothing to do." Repression of anger is ultimately much more harmful to the marriage than an occasional marital explosion that clears the air.

By now some readers may be concluding that it is being argued that any anger, whether major or minor, should always be expressed. Not at all. Only a child does this. Anger, like any other human emotion, including love, must be disciplined and channeled. There are some people who need to learn to keep more anger inside, and others who need to get more out. Frank Selph was one such thirty-five-year-old "child" who had yet to learn how to discipline his anger. Every irritation was a major occurrence to him, especially when he was home. His wife reported, and he confirmed her story, that recently he had been carrying wood for the fireplace from the car into the house and dropped a piece on his foot. He flew into a rage (tantrum?), picked up the wood and broke out every window in the car, and for good measure went to the front and "blinded" the car by bashing in the headlights! This was not the first time he had done this to a car, so she said they always drove an old car.

Though Frank's handling of anger is immature, so is the man who keeps all his anger inside, or the one who is mad at the boss and takes it out on his children, or the wife who is angry with the husband and prepares for supper a casserole she knows he detests. These are but a few of the abortive ways of handling anger.

CHRISTIANITY AND ANGER

There appears to be a widespread opinion that there is something antithetical about being a Christian and feeling and expressing anger. As a teen-ager, I once mentioned to a minister about getting angry with some friends. The minister promptly offered to pray on the spot for that sinful and wayward lad! I was sinful all right, but my anger had contributed little or nothing to that condition! Nonetheless, this discomfort reflects a feeling on the part of some Christians that if they were "closer to the Lord" or more dedicated to the Christian cause, they would experience no anger. The truth of the matter is that dedicated Christian husbands and wives do get angry with each other. Their Christian faith has not exempted them from undergoing the same discipline for building a meaningful relationship that any other husband and wife must undergo. This also includes what is often a painful working through their areas of conflict in both quarrels and calmer discussions. At the same time, a meaningful religious faith can provide an additional resource of strength in helping couples resolve their conflicts.

Eleanor Morrison, in an excellent article on family anger, says that these "If-You-Practice-Christianity-There-Will-Never-Be-Any-Disagreement" Christians are unlike the apostle Paul because "they think that which they would do is attainable and simple and that which they would not do can be quickly denied and vanquished." ("Family Peace at Any Price?" *International Journal of Religious Education,* May, 1967, p. 37.)

As a matter of fact, Paul had some rather interesting comments on anger. In Eph. 4:26 he admonishes his readers: "Be ye angry and sin not." Be angry? Yes! It seems that what he is saying is that there is a type of anger which, rather than being sinful, is in fact desirable. That is, some anger rather than alienating people, rather than being destructive and isolating, is instead constructive, upbuilding, and contributes toward demolishing the barriers of alienation and separation.

Paul hastens on in the same passage to say, "Let not the sun go down upon your wrath." What does he mean? I think he means this: Just as surely as the setting sun draws to a close another day, even so let it also draw to a close the anger and irritation that has built up during the day. Why? Otherwise the new day not only opens up on yesterday's anger but also adds its own. We often see those people on whose anger the sun never sets. Five years after something occurred, they can still become as angry as the day it happened and may still be throwing it up to the mate. So it drags on month after month and year after year, because the sun never sets on their anger. Paul is recognized as a great theologian, but in this passage he voices a profound psychological truth as well.

People who never let the sun set on their anger usually engage in what George Bach calls "gunnysacking." (*The Intimate Enemy,* p. 4.) That is, they simply tuck unresolved bits of anger in the backs of their minds. One can easily do a certain amount of this without much difficulty, but when the gunnysack gets full of dozens and dozens of angry memories and experiences, it ruptures. The stench of rotting anger has polluted more than a few marriage relationships.

Those who view anger as being unchristian need also to remember that it was Jesus who, angered over abuses in the Temple, drove the money changers out. However, some avoid the use of the word "anger" here and say that he became "righteously indignant."

MODES OF HANDLING ANGER

What do you do with your anger? The answer to this question is vitally important, for how a person handles his anger largely determines how he gets along at home, with friends, and at work. In fact, it may determine whether he has any work at all! In premarital counseling, one area I regularly explore with a couple has to do with ways in which they typically handle anger. Hopefully, their courtship has been adequate and open enough for them to be emotionally honest with each other when irritated or angered by the other. Such couples are already at work discovering meaningful ways of coping with anger. Other couples hide behind the smiling mask of courtship, and only after marriage does the angry and often snarling self become manifest.

There is much that we do not know about the reasons why one person responds in anger to a situation while another responds in quite a different manner. However, for the most part, the way we handle anger is probably a learned behavior. As David Abrahamsen notes, if a child grows up in a home characterized by parents who express wild and uncontrolled anger, then that child too is likely to handle anger similarly in adulthood. It is the dominant parent he says, who sets the pattern. (*The Road to Emotional Maturity,* pp. 358–368.) On the other hand, a child may grow up in a home in which no expressions of anger are permitted, and in which he is made to feel guilty over showing anger. He, then, in adulthood is likely to handle his anger in a similar repressive manner.

Anger expresses itself in varying and often mystifying ways. But express itself it will. Anger always leaves a footprint. It can be denied, repressed, and camouflaged, but somewhere the telltale footprint of its presence is recorded. One wife reported that she never got angry with her husband; that upon feeling "put out" with him, she did the ironing. And that is her footprint—ironing. There must be something therapeutic about slapping a searing iron onto a piece of cloth, especially if it happens to be the seat of the husband's trousers!

Some common modes of handling anger will be discussed briefly:

1. The *Volcano* is one way of coping with anger. This person's anger is quiet, sometimes for months at a time. But all the while he has been "gunnysacking" his anger. He can absorb a lot of frustration. Then the family begins to sense that something is about to blow. Days before the explosion the "ground rumbles." Then one day on the slightest provocation the volcano erupts and spews hot lava over the countryside. During these times the family "heads for the hills," because a volcano may become violent physically, and the person is certain to hurl the fire and brimstone of cutting and searing words.

Every few months the newspaper carries a news item of some obedient, quiet, model child who suddenly without warning and apparent reason erupts in violence and murders his parents or someone else. This child, like a volcano, is able to repress the inferno of his anger for years and gloss over his behavior with the kind of conformity that may cause neighbors to view him as an ideal child. Finally, the pressure of unexpressed anger becomes too much and it explodes in death.

2. A second way of handling anger is what I call the *Bean Pot*. This person, like the Volcano, keeps anger inside, but it is poorly concealed. You know that the steam of anger is there, because you can see the lid on the pot lifting! There are several types of Bean Pots. The sulker and the pouter are two of them. The sulker may not speak to other members of the family for days at a time. When queried as to what is wrong, the sulker replies gruffly: "Nothing, nothing! Can't a person be quiet a little without you thinking he is a psychiatric case?" The Bean Pot does not come out openly and say, "I'm mad at you!" Rather, this type of person lets anger brew and stew inside and punishes the family by silence, by withholding love, and by refusing to cooperate with family members.

3. The *Blowtorch* is an extremely difficult person with whom to live. At all times these persons are burning, and anyone having to relate very closely to them, whether in marriage or at work, will surely get burned before long. Basically, the Blowtorch is "mad at the world." Anger always lurks just below the surface. These persons seek acceptance, love, and warmth, but consciously or unconsciously always expect to be hurt, deceived, taken advantage of. They are never disappointed. Their expectation becomes a kind of self-fulfilling prophecy. This always ends in anger and disappointment, during which they may incinerate the object of their anger.

4. The *Big Joker* never handles anger toward a person by saying he or she is angry. Rather, the Big Joker handles hostilities by constantly joking, kidding, teasing, ribbing—at someone else's expense. Those who have been around such a person know that often, after experiencing the sting of a particular tease, they discover that a few drops of "psychic blood" have been drawn.

Faye Williams was married to a Big Joker. At gatherings he looked upon himself as the life of the party, though some others found him to be a bore with his constant joking and teasing. "He never gets serious," reported one person. Big Joker Williams had many grievances against Faye, but he seldom got them out into the open. However, she reported that invariably at a party he told his favorite joke about the oft-divorced wife. The punch line of the joke was, "Honey, your problem isn't getting a man; it's keeping him!" Big Joker would double up with laughter. Faye never laughed. She knew he was deliberately irritating her because he was aware that she was sensitive about his being her third husband.

If Big Joker's hand is called and an objection to the joking is made, this person becomes indignant: "Look, don't be so thin-skinned. Boy, you must be really insecure! Can't you take a little teasing?"

5. *Kick the Dog* is one of the more favorite ways of expressing anger. As the clichéd story goes: He was mad at the boss, but went home and kicked the dog. Of course, that is safer, especially if the dog is tied! Wives may play Kick the Dog when angry with the husband, but instead take it out on the children. An excellent example of displaced anger (the psychological term for this phenomenon) was found in a couple who sought counseling. The husband was a demanding, domineering, insensitive man. On

the other hand, the wife was a quiet, submissive, sweet person who never seemed to get angry with her husband. The counselor was puzzled as to what she did with her anger toward such an irritating and difficult man as the husband. After much exploration this quiet, submissive little wife privately confided to the counselor that for years, every morning after the husband went to work, she has taken his toothbrush and swished it several times in the bathroom commode! So far as is known, she is still swishing it each morning.

6. *Too-Mature-to-Fight* handles anger in another way. These persons view anger as an expression of immaturity. They are not immature. They like to think that they have outgrown the need to express anger. They like to believe that their marriage is such that they have moved beyond quarrels, and they may have been successful in so completely repressing anger that they honestly do not feel anger. However, as stated earlier, anger never leaves without making a footprint. One couple boasted that in thirty years of marriage they had never had a quarrel. Yet, both had such upset stomachs that neither could eat many foods. The doctor could find no physical basis for the malady and concluded that it was psychosomatic. In this case, each apparently, literally, gave the other a "pain in the stomach."

The anger of Too-Mature-to-Fight may also express itself in other camouflaged ways: depressions that seem to have no real basis, headaches, digestive upsets, back and neck pains, undue fatigue, or one of many other ways. (Note that these *may* be due to some psychological cause. They may also be due to a physical dysfunction, so a physician should always be consulted about such conditions.)

It has been said that a person can swallow a lot more anger than he can digest. The psychological and physical problems of Too-Mature-to-Fight are graphic evidence of this fact.

7. *Senator Foghorn* is an old and respected fighter who has survived many campaigns. Whereas Bean Pot handles anger by silence, Senator Foghorn believes in demolishing the enemy with a barrage of words. He (though Senator Foghorn may be a she) is glib of tongue and agile of mind. When angered he strikes out with words. The noise of words is his potent weapon. He may pontificate mightily and speak with much more certainty and authority than his confidence and experience merit. Being handy with words, he can argue with his wife that the world is shaped like a triangle and seem to come out the winner. On those rare occasions when she is about to corner him in an argument, he has a host of ploys to avoid being pinned. He may (*a*) filibuster—"Don't talk, just listen to me"; (*b*) pick up an insignificant detail in the quarrel and switch the subject to that area—"How did we get off on this?"; (*c*) engage in semantics—"Define what you mean by love."

There are certainly other ways of expressing anger. Perhaps you can think of some. Of course, no person handles all his anger in one way. Usually several methods are used. As one husband asked the author, "What do you do if you are married to a joking, volcanic pot of beans?"

CONSTRUCTIVE AND DESTRUCTIVE MARITAL QUARRELS

An early family specialist, Willard Waller, was one of the first to see in a marital quarrel the possibility of something positive. Consequently he distinguished between constructive and destructive quarrels. (*The Family: A Dynamic Interpretation,* p. 353.) In a destructive quarrel one or both mates engage in name-calling or other such practices, so that the relationship is in a worse state at the conclusion of the quarrel than before the couple started. On the other hand, in a constructive quarrel the couple may become quite angry with each other and engage in shouting, but by the time the quarrel is concluded, understanding the other's point of view has occurred, issues have been clarified, and perhaps agreement has been reached on future handling of the issue under consideration. The end effect is that the whole relationship has been strengthened. A person recognizes that it is sometimes difficult to keep an argument from degenerating from a constructive into a destructive one.

George Bach, as noted earlier, is the leading contemporary exponent of constructive marital quarrels. His book *The Intimate Enemy* carefully discusses how to quarrel with your mate—and win too! While there are some preliminaries to be considered in marital fighting, the actual fight, according to Bach, proceeds through several "rounds" something as follows: The wife, let us say, begins round 1 by announcing that she is mad and wants to fight. She may not say it in those words, but she is unmistakably clear in getting that point across. Round 2 begins with her announcing what has made her angry. In round 3 the husband "reads back" to her what he understands her to be angry about. This permits them to fight about the same thing. In round 4 she corrects him if necessary or adds whatever she thinks is needed to her grievance. In subsequent rounds, which may number as many as twenty-one, their anger continues to be expressed, but each is also coming to some understanding about the other. There may be some bargaining in final rounds ("If I try to get home from work on time, will you stop telling the kids how their father is gone all the time?"), and, if possible, they come to some agreement about future actions.

According to Bach, in a good marital quarrel, each mate serves as a referee. For instance, if the above husband says, "Don't think you're going to boss me around like your mother has your father for thirty-five years," she calls a foul! They are not fighting about her parents. If he wants to fight about that, come back tomorrow!

Another important rule in marital quarreling, Bach states, is avoiding "hitting below the belt." All people have areas about which they are sensitive. Most women are sensitive if overweight. To strike there in anger regardless of the subject of the quarrel is hitting below the belt. It hurts her and is irrelevant to the quarrel. Mates need to let each other know where the "beltline" is, since often one is unaware that the other is sensitive about certain areas.

As printed here, such arguments sound very mechanical, stilted, and even ludicrous. Yet, were one to perform an "autopsy" on a successful quarrel, one would likely find that the couple is basically following the outline. That is, there is an unmistakable "declaration of war"; the issue is clarified; they quarrel about that issue only and end up having resolved something.

Most creative quarrels probably begin much like gasoline thrown on a fire: there is an initial flash of anger and for a few moments or minutes the flames burn high. But gradually tempers cool, and the couple settles into a calmer discussion of the issues at hand.

Whether a fight will be constructive or destructive is determined by the degree to which the husband and wife involved care about each other and genuinely wish to deepen their relationship by working through their conflict. On the other hand, if the basic desire is to win, to draw blood, to put the other one in his place, then nothing will be accomplished other than having become a little more alienated from each other. Undergirding a constructive quarrel is a basic commitment to each other in respect, loyalty, and trust. In and through it all, the motivating force is the desire to come into deeper communication, or communion, with the mate.

Learning the Lesson of Forgiveness

While learning to express anger adequately is important to a meaningful marriage, learning to forgive is also important. Forgiveness is a necessary part of the fabric of all human relations. Forgiveness is needed, because once hurt has been inflicted, once something has been said or done, it cannot be changed or called back. Even though a couple works through a major problem, there is the danger of old wounds reopening to infect the marriage. For instance, a husband may come to understand the reasons why his wife became involved with another man. But he still frets over the other man on occasion. During these times he wants to go over the whole painful affair with her once again. This is beginning to get old to her. Forgiveness can help resolve such a problem. Interestingly, marriage counselors have yet to devote much attention to the importance of forgiveness in helping couples to work through their problems.

This discussion of forgiveness is made in the full awareness that, as someone has said, "True forgiveness is one of the rarest of human achievements." Forgiveness does not mean that one literally forgets what happened. How can such hurt be forgotten? (It may be "forgotten" through repressing the hurt, but repression is not forgiveness.) Rather, forgiveness means that the sting has been removed from the hurt. Forgiveness does not remove the bomb; instead, it removes the fuse so that it is not constantly threatening to explode and thus endanger the relationship.

It is at the point of forgiveness that couples with a vital religious faith have a resource available to them that others do not have. For if a Christian man and a Christian woman have both experienced God's forgiveness, then they have another basis on which to forgive each other.

For those of you who have sometimes been uncomfortable because your marriage has been punctuated by periodic quarrels, rejoice that you can quarrel! Evelyn Duvall notes that the everyday world is organized in such a manner that the frank expression of anger is not permitted. The employee who tells his boss what he really thinks of him may not get promoted and could even lose his job. Consequently the individual is forced to control his annoyances in our industrial society. In the face of this enforced hypocritical mode of living she says:

> There needs to be some place, however, where the individual can give vent to his annoyances and be himself, and that place seems to be in marriage. If there is that kind of cantankerousness in a marriage, the couple should chalk it down as proof that their marriage is performing one of its main functions—providing a place to let off steam and re-establish emotional balance. If a marriage is so fragile that it must be maintained by the same artificial manners that keeps an office force functioning, it is pretty precariously based. (*When You Marry,* p. 242.)

Duvall concludes this refreshing passage by quoting one authority as saying, "One of the functions of marriage is to weave a rope of relationship strong enough to hold each person at his worst."

Chapter 4

MONEY, MEANING, AND MARRIAGE

Money! The word rings in our minds like the bell on a cash register. However, because the research of Emily Mudd, Blood and Wolfe, and others indicate that money is one of the top battlegrounds for marital quarrels, it may be that the bell is the one kept at ringside signaling time for another round in the marital bout. Whichever bell it is, its sound triggers various emotional reactions in the American breast.

The term "battleground" used above was done so calculatedly. That is, the money quarrels that unhappy couples bring to marriage counselors are rather infrequently the *real* problems. Rather, money is simply the battleground over which they fight about unspoken, and sometimes unconscious, deeper-lying issues. Seldom does the problem seem to be that they really do not have enough money to meet their *necessities*. American couples quarrel, to a large degree, over how to spend their *surplus* money, i.e., money not needed for necessities. (This perhaps would not be true for low-income families, who realistically do not have enough money to provide an adequate standard of living.)

If the amount of money is not the real problem with ordinary American families, what is the problem? The problem focuses at two primary points: husbands and wives have *unrealistic* and *immature* attitudes about money. That is, they have allowed money to develop hidden, emotional meanings in which it becomes a means for controlling others, of expressing or withholding love, of punishing a mate, of compensating for personal inadequacies, or one of several other meanings.

In this chapter we will consider some of these hidden meanings and explore some of the ways in which people handle money.

WHEN MONEY ISN'T MONEY

There are times when money isn't money. Rather, it is a symbol for other realities. Money in its healthiest sense is simply a medium of exchange. It is seen as having a specific value capable of purchasing a specific object or service. That is all. Unfortunately, money can and does develop other meanings. Sigmund Freud and the late Edmund Bergler were among the first to write on this symbolic use of money. Bergler's book *Money and Emotional Conflicts,* first published in 1951, continues to be the best single treatise on the emotional and neurotic uses to which money is put. At the conclusion of his first chapter, Bergler outlines seven major differences between what he calls the "normal" and the neurotic uses of money (pp. 18–19).

First, Bergler says that money is normally simply a means to an end, the end of acquiring a desired product or service. Neurotically, money becomes an end in itself. This person, like Silas Marner, may become a miser to hoard and collect money for money's sake. He may derive great joy from perusing his savings account book, counting his money, or handling his stocks and bonds.

Secondly, Bergler says that normally a person will not allow himself to be taken advantage of in financial matters. He will take precautions to prevent this, but he does not become preoccupied with the matter. On the other hand, the neurotic lives in fear of being cheated, swindled, short-changed, or otherwise being taken advantage of in financial matters. This fear gets exaggerated out of all proportion to the danger itself. The neurotic is sure that everyone is out to separate him from his money by some devious method.

Thirdly, normally a person will try to make as much money as he can. However, he is not so obsessed with making money that he is willing to sacrifice his family, love, hobbies, or personal contentment to achieve this goal. But to a person who has a neurotic attitude toward money, the acquisition of money becomes the central focus of life, the prime mover. Everything else—health, love, hobbies, recreation, and contentment—is subordinated to the urge to possess more and more money. This husband will ignore all the distress signals of a floundering marriage, because of the lack of time, attention, and love in order to make more money. He will take on extra projects, take all the overtime he can get, or take a second job when he really does not need the money to maintain a reasonable standard of living.

Fourthly, a healthy attitude toward money assumes that ultimately it will be spent. And, as Bergler says, it requires no special surgical operation to put a dollar into circulation. But to a money neurotic, the hoarding and collecting of money becomes the predominant motif of life. Separating him from his dollar is difficult and creates great anxiety within him.

Fifthly, a person who has a healthy attitude toward

money at times must of necessity reject unnecessary requests for money. And this is done in a matter-of-fact way. But to someone who has a neurotic attitude toward money, such requests or demands for money generate anger, excitement, and indignation. This person cannot give a simple no to the request.

Sixthly, Bergler says that normally money has no infantile strings attached to it. It is given without any hidden pleas, requests, or conditions attached. Neurotically, however, money is a blind for existing repressed infantile needs and conflicts. Thus, the neurotic gift of money conceals the plea, "Now, please love me," or perhaps the command, "Now, you have to love me."

Lastly, Bergler says that the statement, "I can't afford it," is a simple statement of fact to one with a healthy attitude toward money. But to the money neurotic, the phrase represents a "defensive triumph against psychic masochism." The neurotic derives some satisfaction from refusing himself something. In fund-raising campaigns we are urged to "Give until it hurts," and it takes little giving to hurt the money neurotic.

In these seven healthy and neurotic attitudes toward money as outlined by Bergler, it should be noted that no one of us entirely escapes being somewhat tainted by neurotic attitudes toward money. To be sure, some people seem to have more than their share of distorted ideas and attitudes about money. But one does not have to look too far within oneself to find some elements of neuroticism toward money. It may be as harmless as the wife who works hard cleaning her house so that she can go to the coffee shop and buy herself a milk shake. Otherwise she feels a bit guilty buying one, as if she doesn't merit it.

Marriage counselors have noted that there is often a

connection between the kind of conflicts a couple has and the way the partners handle their money. The behavior patterns of each partner tend to be reflected in the way each copes with money. Thus, for example, it is not uncommon to find that conflicts over impulse spending reflect a tendency on the part of one or both mates in other ways to impulsively "want what they want" without working together as a team.

An examination of marital money quarrels usually reveals that money as a battleground is a less threatening or a safer area on which to vent hostilities than the deeper-lying issues. Money is a more socially and emotionally acceptable area on which to displace the stored-up resentments than if the real issues were faced openly and honestly.

Let us turn now to some of the common, everyday ways in which husbands and wives express their money conflicts.

SOME COMMON FAMILY ATTITUDES TOWARD MONEY

One characteristic of humans is that all we possess tends to take on secondary or symbolic meanings. That is, an automobile at its most basic level is simply a means of transporting ourselves from one place to another. But an automobile from earliest times has developed other symbolic meanings. It symbolizes success, prestige, freedom, independence, even masculinity. Vance Packard in *The Hidden Persuaders* notes that a convertible is a mistress symbol to men.

Just as an automobile or clothes develop secondary

meanings, even so does our money develop other meanings. It is the purpose of this section of the chapter to discuss some of the common attitudes that husbands and wives have toward money and how these manifest themselves in the family.

1. The first attitude is the *"Bathroom Towel"* attitude —His and Hers. This attitude occurs in families in which both the husband and the wife are employed and one or both insist on keeping the money they earn separate from the other. This practice has some inherent risks. When the Wilsons married it was agreed that Mrs. Wilson would continue to work as a teacher until they decided to start a family. She opened a separate checking account, and they agreed that she would buy her clothes out of her income and would bank the rest. This worked well for a while. Their first big quarrel occurred the following June immediately after her school was out and they were planning for their summer vacation. While the husband's income was sufficient for their usual expenses, it was hardly enough for the vacation too. So he suggested that his wife withdraw three hundred dollars from her account for the vacation. She indignantly refused. This was her money, and if he did not have enough money for the vacation, he could borrow it from his company's credit union.

This kind of situation usually reflects the need on the part of the wife to assert her own independence. At the same time she uses her money to exercise control over the husband. It may also be her way of retaliating for some real or imagined hurt from the husband.

It is difficult to know whether separate bank accounts are a reflection of or a cause of a lack of "we-ness" in a family. In any case, money is such a powerful symbol in our society that it is probably difficult for most couples to handle separate accounts skillfully. Separate accounts tend to contribute to a "my money" and "your money" attitude in the home instead of "our money." Unless a couple has good reason for it, it is doubtful that the risks of separate accounts are worth the advantages.

2. A second approach to money is the *"I'll pick up the check"* attitude. You can always count on this person picking up the check. He will even make a scene over the matter. The truth is he *needs* to pay the check. This exhibitionistic spender has a need to impress others with his affluence, or his generosity. More importantly, he has a need to bolster his own ego, to reassure himself of his importance and success.

Mr. and Mrs. "I'll pick up the check" also find other ways of using money to bolster their egos. They surround themselves with expensive "adult toys," such as boats, stereo record players, cameras, tape recorders, flashy cars, color televisions, and clothes with "proper" (i.e., prestigious) labels attached. They enjoy attending class reunions, conventions, and paying visits to relatives and old friends "back home," since this provides an excellent opportunity to display all that their money has bought and thereby impress others (and themselves) with how successful they have been.

This kind of ostentation is one of the major motivations to which advertisers appeal. And it always works with Mr. and Mrs. "I'll pick up the check."

3. The *"Commanding General"* attitude is held by those who view money as the key to controlling others. Although both men and women may use money as a means of commanding control of others, husbands in particular are likely to use money this way. In this case, it becomes a way of asserting, affirming, and commanding dominance and

control over others—perhaps the wife.

Guy Smithers was such a husband. Mrs. Smithers told the marriage counselor that she had no idea how much money her husband made, what his investments were, or how much savings they had. He deposited a fixed amount in her checking account each month, out of which she paid the household bills. Furthermore, he carefully scrutinized the monthly balance sheet from the bank and expected her to account for any money spent on nonroutine items. She complained of feeling treated as a child on an allowance. Mrs. Smithers was extremely unhappy, but felt that her husband's control over the finances made it difficult for her to do much about it.

The "Commanding General" also uses his money to bestow favors upon those who are submissive to his dominance.

Counselors working in university settings often see students whose families continue to use the checkbook to exercise control over their single or married children. The parents of one married student even continued sending a monthly check after their son had told his parents that he and his wife could live without it. When the son objected to his parents' complaining about how much he and his wife ate out, the parents attempted to affirm their control by reminding him that they sent a monthly check. This economic dependence is often enough to squelch any signs of independence on the part of a son or daughter. Fortunately, in this case, the son thereafter returned the monthly checks—much to the parents' consternation. You see, they *needed* to give him money. Without it, Mr. "Commanding General" had no more control over his son.

4. *"Here's a dollar's worth of love"* attitude is found in those families where one or both partners think love, like

other things in their lives, can be purchased for the price of the dollar. It is true that money can purchase books, looks, automobiles, sex, and companionship. It often is able to attract (purchase?) a mate. But money is no substitute for love.

Bill Elsworth was a rather rigid, undemonstrative man who seemed to have difficulty establishing or tolerating close, intimate relationships. Patty, his wife, complained that he rarely seemed to take a personal interest in her or express any feelings of love—unless he was interested in sex. Yet, Bill rather regularly brought Patty gifts of jewelry, clothes, and perfumes. When in a quarrel she complained that their house was an emotional desert, he became angry and reminded her of the gifts. "I notice you haven't turned down any of my gifts," he said accusingly. "But don't you see," she responded, "I want you, not your gifts." These ideas are incomprehensible to men such as Bill Elsworth.

Mr. "Dollar's worth of love" is a person who is also likely to spend little time with his children. He is making money. He is busy "getting to the top." To compensate for this lack, or inability to give himself, he may shower the children with expensive gifts, stereo record players, motorcycles, sports cars, or generous allowances.

Mr. "Dollar's worth of love" seems to see himself as having nothing worth bestowing on his family except another dollar. Illness, retirement, or loss of his job hit him especially hard, for they strike at his most critical point—his ability to earn a dollar. Since he tends to see all things as being measured by the value of a dollar, and since his own identity is so closely tied to the dollar mark, he feels useless and worthless. No longer can he offer a "dollar's worth of love." He has nothing to offer.

But sometimes it is the wife who equates the spending of money with love. In this case, she tends to gauge the degree of her husband's love for her by how many dollars he spends on her. Or she may drive him to earn more money, which means he can spend more on her. One husband reported being under pressure from his wife to take on a second job so they could buy more. Then she complained that he did not spend enough time with her!

Of course, some husbands do not express love in the usual ways or by giving gifts. The wife of one such husband complained that he never brought her gifts or told her that he loved her. His response in the counselor's office was: "Look, didn't I tell you I loved you when we married? Well, until you receive further notice, that still stands!"

5. The *"Save for a rainy day"* attitude is held by those who live under the constant fear of impending financial doom—the loss of a job, economic depression, illness, or accident. Consequently, these people *oversave*.

For example, Helen Rice grew up during the years of the Great Depression. More than thirty years later she recalls with great vividness her ragged clothes, the toyless Christmases, and her father's crying over the family's poverty. She lives in fear of another similar occurrence. She constantly hounds her husband to save more money even though they have a year's salary in savings. Of course, this is considerably more than the reserves usually recommended for a family.

6. Related to the above is the *"Pack Rat"* attitude toward money. This person does not seem to be reacting to any particular past deprivation, nor is he saving for anything in particular. Mr. "Pack Rat" simply enjoys collecting money. This type of person is occasionally reported in

the newspapers. Some "destitute" old man dies and the police find thousands of dollars packed away in closets, suitcases, and paper bags. To get a "pack rat" to spend his money sometimes makes him almost paranoid. He may assume that everyone, including, or especially, his wife, is trying to get his money.

7. On the opposite end of the continuum is the *"Don't save it for your kids to fight over"* attitude. Rather than oversaving, this person *overspends*. This overspender will sometimes make a joke (he thinks) about how he is going to enjoy his money rather than save it for his kids to fight over after he dies.

As a matter of fact, the overspender is often trying to compensate for past deprivations. Some who grow up in destitute circumstances seem bent on a frenzied attempt to make up for all their past privations and buy all the things they feel they missed as children. This leads them deeper and deeper into debt as they pursue their impulses for the trinkets of an affluent society.

Unfortunately, such spending often leads people into entirely unrealistic purchases. For instance, one young couple of limited means purchased a vacuum cleaner that cost nearly four hundred dollars from a door-to-door salesman. It was a good vacuum cleaner. However, all they had to clean were some throw rugs! Another man bought an expensive piece of shop equipment that made into several different tools. It too was an excellent piece of equipment. Except in this case he knew nothing about woodworking and, further, had no real interest in learning.

Modern easy purchasing at the flash of a credit card is a source of concern to many family counselors. They feel that easy credit contributes to leading persons with more immature and unrealistic attitudes about money into impulse gratification that they might otherwise avoid. "Buy now, pay later" is the gospel of modern high-pressure salesmanship. This gospel offers to us all the chrome-plated baubles and bangles of our plants and factories at the mere flash of the ubiquitous credit card.

Since so many of the present young marrieds have grown up in affluence where most of their hearts' desires were easily gratified, this "now generation" also wants to get married now and move into a house of their own now, have new furniture now, own a new car now. And instant gratification is made relatively easy by "easy" credit. This may be a source of irritation to their parents and grandparents, who remind the young couple that they worked years before they acquired these things—much to the irritation of the young couple.

Unfortunately what Mr. and Mrs. "Don't save it for your kids to fight over" confront is that they may not have enough for the children *now* once they make their many monthly payments.

8. The *"Bull Whip"* attitude toward money is the final one to be considered here. In this case, money is viewed as a weapon to crack over the heads of recalcitrant family members. Anyone who fails to fall into line is whipped into submission, with money used as the whip.

A wife who withholds sexually (her weapon) may find Mr. "Bull Whip" retaliating by withholding money from her. Children who are disobedient have their allowances withheld by Mr. and Mrs. "Bull Whip." One of the main reasons why family specialists usually advise against cutting allowances as punishment is that this tends to put a dollar value on conforming behavior. The parent may unwittingly communicate to the child that money and love are tied up together. "When you obey me, I love you more;

I give you your money," may be what the child perceives the parent as saying.

Wives are not beyond using money as a weapon. Otis Wilson was a fine but rather insensitive man who was often critical of women's idea of the importance of being a woman. Margaret, his wife, quite properly resented this. He accused her of being lazy, because she did not want to work outside the home. Interestingly, one of Otis' chief complaints about Margaret to the marriage counselor was that she was extravagant with charge accounts. Furthermore, he had recently counted thirty-seven pairs of shoes in her closet. Exploration of the matter revealed that unconsciously she was using money as a weapon against him. She could not attack him directly for his lack of appreciation for her. But she could hit him where it hurt with the only "bull whip" she felt she possessed—money.

Wealthy families quite regularly are known to hold various family members in line by the use of money. James Knight cites a cartoon (*Saturday Review,* January 30, 1965) that is apropos. In the cartoon an elderly, wealthy man says to his butler: "Harkness, get me my will. I feel like disinheriting somebody." (*For the Love of Money,* p. 71.)

MAKING PEACE WITH MONEY

Money, like fire, is a faithful servant, but a tyrannical master. Because of this, we must either master our money or be forever intimidated and dominated by it. But making peace with money is not easy. The whole business world has conspired together to use every device of our electronic, scientific, psychological age to create within us a desire for its products. More than this, as has already been noted, no one of us entirely escapes having some distorted attitudes about money. We, therefore, cannot view money without a taint of neuroticism.

Although almost any discussion of money management seems to be trite and superficial, perhaps some of the suggestions below might be of help in learning to live at peace with money.

1. The first law of finance is that a person must live within his income. It is possible to spend $1,000 this month on an $800 income and get away with it. One may even get away with doing it again next month. But before long, one of the basic laws of finance will settle upon that family: You cannot consistently spend more than you make and get away with it. (One wonders what will ultimately happen to the billions of dollars of Federal Government "overrun" which has now collected as the national debt.)

Over the years I have talked with families in counseling that run the spectrum of family incomes—meager to affluent. I have decided that the size of the income bears little relationship to the amount of financial stress that the family experiences. Many families that make twice the national average have more problems than families that make half the national average. How can this be? The answer lies mainly in the attitudes that people have toward money, and one of the main economic "sins" is to spend more than one makes.

2. Family finances require family cooperation. Since the whole family is involved in spending—husband, wife, children—any realistic attempt to live within an income must include the cooperation of the entire family. The family's spending pattern must command everyone's loyalty

and, therefore, must satisfy every family member as being fair. Such a plan is not possible unless there is family co-operation and a willingness to change the plan from time to time to keep it in line with changing family needs.

To be sure, no two families will spend their money exactly the same way. Each family will develop its own techniques for family money planning. The point being made here is that if the plan is to work, the planning should be done by the family, not by one individual. There are few, if any, husbands or wives who can herd the family in one night and announce *ex cathedra* that from now on there will be strict adherence to a plan they have previously drawn up. If the husband carefully plans what he spends while the wife still purchases the choicest cuts of steak, it may help, but it will not help enough.

3. If you are in financial straits, perform an "autopsy" on your spending habits. Careful examination of where your money goes will sometimes reveal places where cuts and savings can be made. This may necessitate keeping a careful record of all money spent for a few months. It is not enough to blame inflation, bad luck, sickness, or circumstances. Something must be *done* to bring outlay more into line with income.

For instance, families often spend unnecessary money on cars. When the car gets old enough to begin needing repairs (and that is soon) the husband may justify buying a new car—which he wants to do anyway—on the basis that it will cost too much to repair the old one. However, for the equivalent of three or four payments on a new car, he can have a rebuilt engine installed in his old car—and save nearly three years' new-car payments.

4. Finally, let the mate who is most adept at the task handle the money. Some men have an idea that the prime

responsibility for the family budget must be theirs—if they are really men. Money is masculine, they feel. And to control the money means to control the family, to be the "head of the house." However, I am not aware of anything written in the stars or in the laws of nature that says a man *ought* to handle the family finances. The reality of the situation is that the wife may be the person who is best equipped temperamentally and otherwise to handle money. She may be less inclined to impulse spending and may have the ability for a total grasp of the family economy. The husband who lacks such a total grasp may look in the checkbook at the end of the month, see that they still have $50, and be tempted to dash out and spend it. What he has difficulty remembering is that the $100 insurance premium is due next month and this will go toward paying that.

"The love of money is the root of all evils," one New Testament writer asserted (I Tim. 6:10). While some people may debate whether the love of money is at the root of all marital evils, we cannot avoid facing the fact that unhealthy and immature attitudes toward money are at the base of many family difficulties. The next chapter will deal with another source of marital conflict—family time.

Chapter 5

FINDING TIME
FOR FAMILY TIME

Mankind has always been intrigued with time. One of his earliest instruments was a device to measure it—the calendar. Though all men experience time, few, if any, can define it. Time mystifies and bewilders man. Though he controls much of the world around him, he cannot control time to either halt, slow, or turn it back. Though he fight it, defy it, resist it, man is inevitably and inexorably swept along in the current of time toward his ultimate destiny. To his dismay and despair he discovers that time, in fact, controls him.

Time, like Death, is no respecter of persons. It metes out to both prince and pauper, the literate and the illiterate, the preacher and the paperhanger, precisely the same amount each day—twenty-four hours.

A major characteristic of time is that it moves in only one direction—forward. So the political candidate is correct when he resorts to that old cliché, "My friends, the future lies ahead of us!" (This may be the only point on which both Democrats and Republicans agree!)

But if politicians, businessmen, and astronomers are concerned with time, we should hasten to say that ordinary families are also concerned with time, but perhaps in a different manner. Rarely do husbands and wives discuss their concerns that the problem of family time is not brought up. "We just don't have time," is repeated again and again. Interestingly, practically no research has been conducted on the subject, and very little has been written. It is the purpose of this chapter to explore this common problem of modern families and then conclude with some suggestions that may be of help in "finding time for family time."

TIME—THE RESIDENT FAMILY ENEMY

"It isn't the spying eye of Big Brother that tyrannizes me, but the pursuing hands of Big Ben!" This confession of a harried housewife could probably be repeated in the homes of most families across the United States. In fact, some family members will tell you that *time* is an academic concept, that only *Time* is real. They insist that Time has a life and a will of its own, that in their home, Time is the resident enemy who relentlessly hounds, pursues, intimidates them.

Should historians search for a symbol to depict our age, I nominate Time's chief henchman, the Clock. So much of our lives seems to be controlled and tied to the clock. A calendar was an accurate enough timepiece for our early forefathers, who measured time in leisurely terms of days, months, and seasons. We measure time in minutes and seconds. A driver who takes five seconds to respond to a green traffic light throws those behind him into fits of irritation. Even the children are affected. If a mother arrives five minutes late to pick up her boy at the swimming pool, she is likely to get scolded for making him wait.

No family seems immune to Time's infectious disease.

I sat in Chicago's O'Hare airport one evening waiting to catch a plane home when I noticed a gentleman nearby reading a book on flying saucers—UFO's. When he put the book aside, I made a comment about the book and mentioned having read that a set of UFO photographs had been proven a hoax. He responded that he knew of this, having been in on the investigation. Surprised, I asked who he was. I immediately recognized his name as that of an international authority on UFO's. We struck up a lively conversation and sat together on the plane, since we both caught the same flight. Upon finding that I was involved in working with families, he began telling me what he considered to be one of his main family problems—Time. He and his wife never seemed to have any time together. Both of them were busy, busy. Then when they did have time, the children were always there. Even when he tried to hug her, a child always seemed to manage to push in between them.

Here was the same story again—no time. Though I knew that ordinary families had this problem and though I know that families are in many ways similar, somehow in a strange way it was reassuring to know that this learned, internationally known scientist had the same problem with time that the rest of us mortals have!

My research with ministers' wives and the problems they confront has been interesting insofar as the matter of family time is concerned. (*The Role of the Minister's Wife,* pp. 79–86.) A series of incomplete sentences on a questionnaire gets interesting responses, particularly the one that reads, "The main thing I dislike about being a minister's wife is . . . " The chief response to that sentence has to do with family time. If "holy smoke" comes out of the parsonage chimney, the blackest of this smoke has to do with smoldering resentments over the lack of family time, particularly family time that can be counted on. As one wife said, "It seems that he's gone all day and all night, and why can't he spend some time with us?" For the husband not to be able to plan to spend, say, Friday evening with the family without fear of having to cancel it is particularly bothersome to many wives. One told me, "Sometimes he decides to take an evening off, but about that time some old biddy will phone with hurt feelings because she wasn't invited to something and it is all off!"

Even the families of counselors are not immune. I was addressing the wives at a church family life conference when a subject came up about which I urged them to talk further with their husbands. One wife in the front row (whose husband was later found to be a counselor) spoke up at that point, and with considerable difficulty maintaining control of her voice asked, "How do you talk with a husband who is never home?" Then, on the verge of tears, she went on to say that her husband was gone all day at work, came in to eat in the evening, and then nearly every night returned to his office or attended some meeting. "I feel as if I am a widow and our children are orphans," she concluded. This wife attended all the sessions of the conference alone—her husband was in New York on business. The danger that confronts family counselors, psychiatrists, and other psychotherapists is that they will "gain the whole world" so far as helping others is concerned but "lose their own souls" at home.

Where Has All the Time Gone?

American men are spending less and less time on the job and more and more time in leisure-time activities. Not only are men spending less time at work, but Mrs. America is also spending less time in traditional housekeeping activities. Washday today is a pleasure compared to what it was in the memory of many women now living. Then there are dishwashers, floor polishers, frozen foods, permanently pressed clothes, and a whole parade of other laborsaving devices. Before the turn of the century Mr. America may have a three-day workweek of ten hours each day. This will give the family a four-day "weekend."

If Americans are having more and more "free" time, where is it going? It doesn't seem to be coming to any of the families known to this writer—certainly not to his own! To be sure, we are spending less time on the job than was spent a generation ago. (This is not to say that some men do not spend as much time as they ever did on the job.) What is happening is that our lives are becoming filled with numerous other activities that are not connected with work but are nonetheless considered important to modern families. Check your own schedule of recent days. What has taken up your time? Committees, church activities, Scouts, music lessons, children's activities, adult education classes, recreational activities, household repairs, and a host of other activities. It is said that nature abhors a vacuum, and this is certainly true so far as time is concerned. Given additional time, Americans will not stretch out on the couch and "rest" it away. Rather, they will find something with which to fill this vacuum of time—and then complain of feeling busy.

In a recent book, *The Harried Leisure Class,* Staffan Burenstam Linder says that people are as busy now using their "free" time as when they spent it at work. He does not see our busyness as changing. He notes that advanced societies have not developed toward an easygoing life of leisure with time for developing man's higher faculties, as some predicted would happen. This, he says, is because the dynamics of economic growth impel men toward a more material existence making things more abundant and time more dear. Consequently, in the future he sees "free" time becoming more scarce, and the American consumer will tend to purchase things that require relatively little of his free time in repairs and relatively more of his income. That is, we will have more money than time.

In our day we are witnessing a change in which leisure time is becoming more and more like work. Observe how feverishly families work at spending their weekends. Talk with those who arrive back home from their summer vacation complaining of needing a vacation to recover from the vacation.

Concern regarding family time is to some degree tied to social class differences. Lower-class families spend relatively little time together as families and are less concerned about the subject. When the men go out, they are likely to go out alone and spend their time in the company of other men. Middle-class America spends the most time together as families, and it is they who complain loudest about the lack of family time.

It is possible that social class uses of time may show up in marital success and failure. This is suggested by the research of John Scanzioni in which he found that women from the laboring class, 8:00 to 5:00 backgrounds who marry "up" the social ladder complain that their husbands work too much and spend too little time with them. On the other hand, women who marry "down" the social ladder complain that their husbands don't work hard enough. (*Ladies' Home Journal,* December, 1968, p. 22.)

This reminds us of another fact of life regarding time: The very factors that contribute to a man's "getting to the top" in his business (long hours, etc.) may mitigate against his being a success at home as a husband and father (at least insofar as time with the family contributes to his success there). Some wives also report that the more their husbands advance career-wise, the less they are able to communicate with them. This is related to the finding of Blood and Wolfe that taking time to talk with the wife about what transpires at work is more characteristic of junior executives than of senior executives. (*Husbands and Wives: The Dynamics of Married Living,* p. 168.)

Sex differences also show up in regard to interest in family time. Family counselors with whom I have talked share my own observation that it seems that the pinch of time is felt more keenly by the wife than by the husband. It is the wife who is most likely to complain about the lack of family time, not the husband. Perhaps this is because he spends more of his time in relationship to others, whereas many of the wives are home without adult companionship. Some support for this is found in my own research with ministers' wives, where those who were employed outside the home were less likely to complain of the loneliness of their roles. This concern on the part of wives may also be a reflection of a difference in the expectations of marriage. To date, we have no large study of the marital expectations of men similar to that which Blood and Wolfe did with women. However, they found that the leading expectation which women have of marriage is companionship (p. 150). Companionship means being together and doing things together. Although this doubtless means much to men, we have some reason to believe that this may play a more important role in the lives of women than of men. Consequently, a wife would be more sensitive to the loss of time with her husband than he would be to a loss of time with her.

One of the complaints that many busy men have is that their wives do not understand how much time their work takes. As a result, they feel that their wives are always trying to extract an extra few minutes of time from them. To these men, their work may be exciting, challenging, and one of the most important things in their lives. They love their wives but do not feel the need to spend that much time with them. Work gets the time. A wife, on the other hand, cannot understand how her husband could love her and yet spend so much time at work, especially when he knows how much she wants him to spend some time with her.

Is there a saturation point in the amount of family time that a couple can comfortably use? There doubtlessly is. One can readily observe this in those couples who can get along fairly well with each other during the week, but who find themselves quarreling on weekends when the husband is home from work. Other couples report trouble when the husband retires and is home all the time. Their wives complain that they are constantly "underfoot." Part of the honest assessment of a couple regarding family time should be some estimate as to how much time they can comfortably use. The truth of the matter may be that they get along much better so long as they do not spend, say, every evening together.

Regardless of whether Americans choose to spend their

time with the family or in other activities, they are aware of the limits put on their nonworking hours. We are coming to regard as precious the finite span of time we spend on this planet, and this is as it should be.

TOWARD FINDING TIME FOR YOUR FAMILY

Finding time for family time is not easy. Time's marching minutes always threaten to force us to spend it in other ways. For those who want to combat the supremacy of the clock, the following suggestions have been helpful to some families:

1. *Decide whether you really want more time together.* This is a basic question. Not all people who say they want more time together really mean it. They might not be able to cope with it. Their filled schedules of work, clubs, and committees may be prima facie evidence that talk about wanting to be with the family more is simply lip service to an idea. Psychologists have a term for those who get involved so as to avoid having to face someone or a situation. They call this "avoidance behavior." Clubs, committees, and work beyond the basic requirements may be simply avoidance behavior. To be sure, all the items in one's repertoire of activities may be worthwhile, important, and seem necessary. But one could work twenty-four hours a day, all in worthy pursuits. The important thing is that this person or this couple have chosen to order their priorities in such a manner that family time comes rather far down the list.

As stated earlier, there is a saturation point in the use of family time. Avoidance behavior of some couples may simply be their unspoken way of taking recognition that more time together would only increase their friction. As it is, they can maintain a reasonably satisfying relationship by avoiding each other and at the same time maintain an illusion with each other that they wish they could be together—if they just had the time.

Other couples genuinely do want to spend more time with each other, but for various reasons have not taken time out to reorder their priorities. It is this group which this chapter is most likely to help.

2. *Reassess your activity schedule.* If your answer to the first item above was "yes," then a second step is to reassess the way your time is spent. Time is much like money; one has only so much "time income" each week— 168 hours. Just as a person has to establish priorities in the expenditure of money, even so does he have to establish a system of priorities in spending his weekly allocation of 168 hours.

How a man chooses to use his time depends on an intricate and obscure complex of motives. Even so, it is possible and necessary for us to pause occasionally and take inventory of the activities that consume our time. An analysis of many of our activities will reveal that they are of secondary importance. One sin of modern man is to expend major energies on minor concerns.

Assuming that one wants to spend more of his free time with the family, how does he go about assessing his schedule? One way of trying to put activities spent away from the family into proper focus is to ask, "If I don't do this, will the world know the difference a month from now, a year, five years?" A sizable percentage of the matters that consume our energies and hound our lives would hardly be missed were we to drop them altogether. This is especially true of "free" time activities in clubs, committees, and other volunteer work.

While the above applies to volunteer work, it is more difficult to know what to do with recreational activities (fishing, hunting, bridge, golf) that take us away from the family. While it may be possible to include family members in some of these, such as fishing, recreational time too must be weighed against the total picture of the demands on one's time. Balance is a hallmark of emotional maturity and balance is needed here. A person should not spend all his time doing only what he enjoys most, but neither should he neglect doing some of those things he enjoys most.

Christian people need also to remember that simply because an event takes place at the church building does not make it an important meeting—it doesn't necessarily make it a Christian meeting. One wife reported that half of her church meetings were meetings to plan other meetings. Some of the people who are at the church every time the doors are open might render a greater Christian service were they to stay home occasionally and invest the time in their families. The New Testament writer's comment that those who fail to look after their own families are worse than unbelievers (I Tim. 5:8) could also apply to those who fail to meet their families' needs for time and attention.

Hordes of Americans are "meeting addicts." They are hooked. One reason many people allow themselves to get so busy is that it enhances their feelings of self-worth. "Look how important I am; everybody wants my attention!" On those rare evenings when a meeting addict has nothing to attend, he will go into "withdrawal symptoms" of anxiety, irritability, restlessness, and perhaps even a headache. Underneath it all is the feeling of worthlessness when forced to stay home. It comes as a real blow to his ego to have to miss some of his precious meetings and discover that the club goes on without missing him.

3. *You must make time for family time.* Those who wait for a free evening to fall into their laps may find themselves waiting and waiting. If time with the family is important at all, it is important enough to make a place for it. Many busy men of my acquaintance schedule time on their appointment books with their wives and families. One professional man regularly blocks out on his schedule the period from 1:00 to 3:00 P.M. every Friday for a long lunch with his wife. If someone calls for an appointment during those hours, he simply tells them that he has a prior appointment. And he does—with his wife! Another man's schedule permits him to have breakfast with his wife after he has spent an hour at work and she has gotten the children off to school.

Parents who do not make time to be with their children usually find that the children extract the time out of them by whining, fighting, or other behavior that demands the parents' attention. True, it is angry attention, but angry attention to a child is often better than no attention.

4. *Work out a time schedule to fit your own family.* This is to say that your family has its own unique needs. In the first place, some families have more need for time together than others. Secondly, each family has to work out a schedule to fit the peculiar interests, personalities, and work schedules of the members. What is meaningful to one family will not be to another. For instance, one way my family enjoys spending leisure time in the summer is to camp out in some beautiful location where we can be close to nature. But a neighbor cannot stand the idea of camping and all the bugs, dirt, and lack of home

conveniences. Excellent! I am aware of no law of nature that says one *should* like to camp. (On the other hand, the way they enjoy spending their leisure time leaves my family cold.) Schedules also differ. A man who works a 3:00 to 11:00 shift obviously must spend his free time differently from one on an 8:00 to 5:00 schedule.

5. *Family time requires family cooperation.* One of the reasons some families have so little time together is that each member insists on doing his "own thing." While this may be desirable in some circumstances, it is hardly conducive to enabling a family to have enough time together to keep the ties of relatedness alive. The wife mentioned above who has lunch with her husband could not do so were he not willing to cooperate and schedule this time with her.

6. *Remember: time is measured in at least two dimensions—quantity and quality.* Let's face it, many busy modern families cannot very realistically have as much time together as, say, a family in which the husband works from 8:00 to 5:00 and is then home for the rest of the evening. But these families can put more *quality* into the time they do have. Thirty minutes spent in which the wife or children have the husband's full attention can be more meaningful than a whole evening together in which the husband and father sits passively in front of the television.

One father of my acquaintance who leads a busy life often has to work at night. Nonetheless, on some evenings he tries to crowd into a few minutes a meaningful experience with his children. One of his rituals is to announce to the children that he is feeling bad and will probably have a "fit." This is a joyous announcement, for the children know that this signals the beginning of a favorite experience. The father feigns passing out, only to recover in a "delirium" and wrestles with the children on the floor, pretending to try to shove one down the stairs while the other tries to rescue the hapless sib. When it is time to go to work he "recovers," claiming to be unable to remember a thing that has transpired. Often ten or fifteen minutes have passed, but they have been memorable ones for the children.

7. *Try to glean the corners of your time.* This Biblical image is derived from the Old Testament requirement that farmers were not to harvest the corners of their fields (Lev. 19:9-10). Rather, the corners were to be left for the poor and the widows. In busy families, there are always some unharvested corners of time that can be put to good use.

The wife of a graduate student complained bitterly of never seeming to have any time with her husband. During the final phases of writing his dissertation he left early in the morning seven days a week and returned for an hour to eat supper, only to leave again until 11:00 P.M. He felt that time was so critical that he could not take off to spend any with her. (Though, as so often happens, she on occasion became so upset that he had to stay home with her. Husbands who do not *give* time to their wives usually have it *extracted* from them.) Finally he suggested that he come home early and they plan to spend from 10:30 to 11:30 each evening together. This was hardly prime time, but it was about the only "ungleaned corner" they could find. She made something a little extra out of these times by baking cookies, pizza, or some other tidbit and they thereby transformed that late hour into a meaningful time together.

Another busy father arrived home one day for lunch and was pounced upon by his children to do something with them. He had only a few minutes, but told the children to go into the backyard and look for beautiful things that are all around them but escape their attention, and he would shortly come out to hunt with them. When he finished a few minutes later and joined the four-year-old and the six-year-old in the backyard, he found two disappointed children who had been unsuccessful in finding even one beautiful thing. Thereupon he walked over and picked a purple flower from a weed growing in a corner. He had each child look at it closely—at the beauty of its color, the shape of the petals, the symmetry of the five petals, and the formations deep down inside it. They had never done this before. Then he picked up a dead leaf from the previous autumn and had the children observe how symmetrically it was formed, with a central vein and branches dividing in all directions. Then he pulled a tender blade of grass and had them look at how the veins ran differently in it. He noted that the edges looked smooth and then had them carefully pull it across the tongue and feel the jagged edges. (Easy. This can cut a tongue!) Then they examined an insect closely. The children found these activities very exciting and spent the next several days searching for hidden beauty. It had all taken ten or fifteen minutes, but this father had gleaned a corner of time and made it into a memorable experience for them all.

No family is so busy that the members cannot find an ungleaned corner of time to harvest. Just as a beautiful flower garden can be created in a small, unused corner of the yard, even so can small, unused corners of time be transformed into miniature holidays for those who know how to cultivate those minutes together.

Deep, meaningful relationships do not flourish in a time vacuum. Love takes time. A danger confronting busy modern families is that in the midst of the many demands made upon their "free" time, their families' cry for time and loving attention will be drowned out. Strangely, those who love us the most often seem to have the least time for us. John Godfrey, the lonely old man in Taylor Caldwell's *The Listener,* expresses this problem well when he says: "Nobody has time to listen to anyone, not even those who love you and would die for you. Your parents, your children, your friends: they have no time. That's a very terrible thing, isn't it? Whose fault is it? I don't know. But there doesn't seem to be any time" (p. 21).

Chapter 6

AVOIDING THE DRY ROT
IN MARRIAGE

At any given moment a thousand diseases threaten to attack and send us to a hospital bed. Although this fact is recognized by the man on the street, he may not realize that his marriage, as well as his body, can become ill by any one of innumerable "marital diseases." Chief among these is marital "dry rot." While the dry rot can prove to be fatal, it more often acts as a low-grade infection that, instead of causing the marriage to become entirely dysfunctional, may prevent the husband and wife from deriving full satisfaction from the relationship.

The term "dry rot" harks back to my boyhood days which were spent growing up on a farm. For use in the home we grew both white and sweet potatoes. As usually happened, some of the white potatoes would rot during the course of their storage, becoming mushy and emitting an offensive odor. On the other hand, sweet potatoes more usually rotted by dehydrating and withering away without any particular odor. Father called this the dry rot. My years as a marriage counselor have convinced me that marriages, like those potatoes, sometimes develop the rot. Some of these dissolve in a big, conspicuous "stink," like the white potatoes. But others seem to, rather quietly and without any particular fanfare, simply wither away. I call this the marital dry rot.

Any marriage can expire in a highly offensive, dramatic, and odorous manner. These are the ones which usually become the gossip of the community and hit the newspapers. Though that kind of rot can attack any family, the attack is more likely to be by the dry rot. Dry rot stalks the door of every marriage. There are no exceptions. Dry rot is an erosive, corrosive, silent, and subtle process in which the relationship between husband and wife gradually begins to wither and dry up. This does not mean that the marriage dies. Instead, like a piece of fine silver the relationship gradually loses some of its luster and becomes tarnished. I believe this process is as inevitable as the turning of the seasons. This is supported by the research of such men as Blood and Wolfe, who found that couples tend to lose touch with each other with the passing of the years. (*Husbands and Wives: The Dynamics of Married Living,* p. 264.) Fortunately, a relationship can be kept alive and vital, but it requires constant work.

Bill and Betty Evans are illustrative of the kind of couple with whom we are concerned in this chapter. They met in high school and married immediately after graduation. They felt that they were deeply in love, and with all the excitement that such young couples have, they plunged into setting up a home. Since Betty worked, they lived comfortably even though they had run up a large debt for furniture and a new car. But Mother Nature had other plans for Betty, and ten months after marriage she became pregnant. Then, as often happens, two more unscheduled babies came along in the next three years. By now the couple was particularly strapped financially, especially since they had hoped Betty could work for the first years to pay off some of their debts. But they tried to face it philosophically and they did enjoy the children. Most people on their block considered them an ideal couple.

By now they found themselves quarreling often—over his work hours, the children, sex, and even little personality traits that at one time had not bothered them. But these quarrels usually passed quickly. Because of the financial situation, they only infrequently got away by themselves. Bill did insist once that they go out for her birthday and he still remembers her announcing in the middle of the meal that she could have bought two dresses for the girls with what it was costing them to go out. She wasn't angry, but that somehow spoiled it for him.

Speaking of clothes, Betty had gained weight with each succeeding baby and now weighed as much as she had during the final weeks of the first pregnancy. Bill would tease her about it, but then would tell her that this just gave him more to love.

Things came to a head one evening when Bill arrived from work and she began telling him about a problem with their son. In anger he yelled at her that he did not want to hear about it. He took care of his problems at work, and why couldn't she take care of hers at home? She shouted back that this was his son too. An overwhelming rage came over Bill, and he found himself grabbing and shaking Betty. Suddenly there was a vast, heavy silence. Never before had he grabbed her in anger. In that silence she broke into floods of tears. His anger was all gone now. He took her into his arms as she repeatedly asked: "What's wrong with us, Bill? What's wrong?"

Bill and Betty's marriage is suffering from the dry rot. Are they unhappily married? Ask them or any one of countless thousands like them, "Would you consider yourself unhappily married?" and they will confidently deny it. And they are not really unhappy; but more importantly, neither are they *really* happy. They are in that limbo of being neither happy nor unhappy. It is a decent existence, but it is just that—an existence. It is with this kind of dry rot that this chapter is concerned.

THREE TYPES OF MARITAL DRY ROT

I have noted three types of dry rot in married couples.

1. *"Marriage is O.K." Dry Rot* is the first to be discussed here. When asked what they think of marriage, this husband or wife is likely to say: "Well, you know, I suppose it is O.K. I wouldn't want to be unmarried, but for the most part I think marriage is overrated." Couples suffering from the "Marriage is O.K." dry rot may not quarrel very much and they put few demands on each other. They are both mutually concerned with the children. Usually the children are the main mutual point of contact that they have with each other. He may be successful in his work and put in long hours there. This means they have little time together as husband and wife, but neither one is particularly bothered by it. They usually have never spent a great deal of time together, even early in their marriage. They both enjoy the monetary rewards of his success at work, though they seldom spend much time discussing the work. She is usually busy in her own activities in church, community, and civic groups. In fact, she is quite busy and often complains of never having time to do anything. But she is always willing to take on an extra committee responsibility. Most of her friends are in these

groups, friends her husband hardly knows. But, on the other hand, neither are his friends and their wives among her close personal friends. Her main contact with them is "duty time," i.e., business entertaining.

The picture that emerges in the "Marriage is O.K." relationship is that of railroad tracks—they run parallel to each other but touch at few points. He is busy and she is busy, but seldom are they busy over the same things.

Cuber and Harroff in their study of differing types of marriages among affluent Americans say that in this type of marriage the couple has no memory of a time when they were close to each other. (*The Significant Americans,* p. 50.) This is the way it has always been. Since this is all they have known, they are likely to assume that all marriages are like this and that vital marriages exist only in the movies and in the minds of hopeless romanticists. They will also be likely to assume that couples who appear to be happy are only putting on an act.

2. The *"Tired Blood" Dry Rot* is a second type. This one is similar to "Marriage is O.K." except at one important point—a "tired blood" couple can remember a time when they were deeply in love with each other, enjoyed each other's company, and shared mutual dreams. But with the passing of the years, they have spent less and less time with each other and their worlds have grown apart as he became immersed in his work and she became involved in her community work and in the rearing of the children. They both continue to be interested in the children and share in certain other interests, but they have lost their ability to really enjoy being in the other's presence. Increasingly they find themselves in need of something to mediate their relationship—guests for dinner, a concert, activities involving the children. No longer do they relish

the opportunity for simply being alone and interacting together.

Cuber and Harroff, cited above, say that a person may react in one of two ways to this type of marriage (which they call "devitalized"): they may fight it, or they may acquiesce (pp. 47–49). Those who fight it may be jealous or resentful of other couples who seem to still enjoy each other. One wife is quoted as saying:

I do know some people—not very darn many—who are our age and even older, who still have the same kind of excitement about them and each other that we had when we were all in college. I've seen some of them at parties and other places—the way they look at each other, the little touches as they go by. One couple has grandchildren and you'd think they were honeymooners. I don't think it's just sex either— I think they are just part of each other's lives—and then when I think of us and the numb way we sort of stagger through the weekly routine, I could scream. (*The Significant Americans,* pp. 48–49.)

On the other hand, a husband or wife may simply acquiesce and drift along with the marital stream. This type is seen in the comments of one wife about her marriage:

Now, I don't say this to complain, not in the least. . . . I'll admit that I do yearn for the old days when sex was a big thing and going out was fun and I hung on to every thing he said about his work and his ideas as if they were coming from a genius or something. But then you get the children and other responsibilities. I have the home and Bob has a tremendous burden of responsibility at the office. . . . He's completely responsible for setting up the new branch now. . . . You have to adjust to these things and

we both try to gracefully. (*The Significant Americans,*
p. 48.)

Obviously, there is more hope for a "Tired Blood" couple
to develop a vital relationship than the "Marriage is O.K."
couple. Since the latter couple has never known anything
different, there is nothing to renew, to recapture.

✓   3. A final type of dry rot is the *"Predisaster" Dry Rot.*
In this marriage, the dry rot has so undermined the relationship that marital disaster is impending. Usually people
involved in this marriage are unaware of how deeply the
"termites" have eaten into the foundations of their relationship. Prior to the disaster, they would likely still consider themselves happily married, if they think of the relationship at all.

A predisaster relationship (and this dry rot could be
viewed as an extension of one of the two previous ones)
has progressed to a point where one or both partners is
open for an emotional involvement with another. Such
emotional entanglements usually begin innocently. John
noticed one day in the company cafeteria that one of the
secretaries from across the hall was eating alone. He went
over and sat down with her. There was a pleasant exchange
during the meal. He talked of his children and she showed
him pictures of hers. (This act is a halfhearted "No Tres-
passing" sign designed to reassure oneself.) It was a pleasant experience. Since they both ate lunch at the same hour,
he made it a point to eat with her the next day, and the
next, and the next. It was all perfectly aboveboard and in
sight of everyone. But unspoken things were happening
within each one of them. Each found the other easy to talk
to, and each seemed interested in what the other had to
say. He particularly liked her sparkling personality. But

he told himself that it was all innocent. By now he was looking forward to lunch. In fact, he found himself waking up in the morning with a new sense of enthusiasm about his work. Life in general had taken on a new glow and for the first time in years he felt as though he had blood coursing through his veins.

By this time he knew he cared more for her than he should. He sensed that she felt the same, though nothing had been said. He found himself suddenly aware that what he took to be a happy marriage to his wife had instead been a dead alliance for years. But by now he had no real desire to try to rebuild a relationship with her. His only thought was for his new love.

For some time John had been a big red apple waiting for someone to come along and shake the tree. The tree was now being shaken, and he, ripe for an affair, was falling. Predisaster had about run its course.

What Causes Marital Dry Rot?

In seeking the causes of dry rot, one should note that the process of decay is a perfectly normal one occurring throughout the world around us. A building begins to deteriorate from the moment it is built. An automobile deteriorates even though it sits unmoved in the garage. Even the mountains decay. Why should we suppose that marriage is immune to these same forces and escapes the need for upkeep? I say this to underline this fact: It is no mark of failure and, indeed, it is to be expected that the dry rot will begin its quiet invasion of any marriage. The marriage can remain alive and vital only by a constant working to keep it that way.

1. One cause of marital dry rot is that the persons in that relationship simply have *difficulty establishing close meaningful relationships*. Marriage has not made them this way. This is particularly true of the "Marriage is O.K." husband and/or wife. Because they likely have been this way much of their lives, change is not so apt to take place as in the "Tired Blood" marriage.

2. A major cause of marital dry rot is *the routine of living*. The "monotony of monogamy" is often spoken of. As with most such statements, it contains some truth. Routine tends to blunt the satisfaction of any experience, partly because one comes to take it for granted and partly because monotony becomes boring. Perhaps you are one who enjoys having his back scratched. When your mate starts scratching, it feels so good! But if the mate continues to scratch in the same spot, it quickly becomes annoying and finally irritating.

Marriage demands that couples work constantly to avoid the kind of routine that can give way to dull, monotonous living. We occasionally need experiences to push us out of the routine of living. Some military families tell me that one fringe benefit of the occasional separations necessitated by military life (unpleasant as these are) is that it shoves them out of their rut and there is a kind of honeymoon effect upon the husband's return.

3. *Being taken for granted* is another cause of marital dry rot. Of course, this is related to the preceding point. Being taken for granted means that a husband and wife fall into such a predictable routine that each is hardly aware of what the other is contributing to the family. This gives rise to a cessation of appreciation for the mate. Being taken for granted makes it possible for a husband to sit at a table spread sumptuously with delicious food attractively served

by his wife, yet never make any complimentary or appreciative remark to her. Should she ask, "Do you like the dinner?" with that quality of voice which wives project when seeking a compliment, he may answer, "Sure, I'm eating it, aren't I?"

4. A fourth factor contributing to marital dry rot is *unrealistic marriage expectations*. In our society, the glories of love and marriage are extolled in song, film, stage, television, novel, newspaper, and magazine. According to the mythology of marriage, in the wedded bliss of matrimony lonely men and women find relatedness, immature kids grow into adulthood, drunken men are reformed, women of easy virtue become sacrificing mothers, and rootless and shiftless men suddenly become stable and responsible fathers. As one student said, "Marriage is something that makes you feel good all over!" The student knows that this is so because she, along with the rest of society, is bombarded with this philosophy from every corner. "We have set up marriage and children," says family specialist Judson Landis, "as the panacea guaranteeing happiness and security to every youngster." (*Life,* August 10, 1962, p. 62.)

When the fires of passion and the halo of romance wear off and the realities of marriage begin to come into focus, many couples feel disillusioned. Some conclude that they are no longer in love. The research of Peter Pineo suggests that men more than women suffer from this disenchantment with marriage. Men are also more disillusioned by sex in marriage than women. ("Disenchantment in the Later Years of Marriage," *Marriage and Family Living,* February, 1961, p. 10.)

A Test for Marital Dry Rot

Before discussing coping with dry rot, perhaps we should pause for what one of my friends calls a "thousand-mile checkup." Below are certain symptoms that may indicate an invasion by the "fungus" dry rot, suggesting a need to "spray" for it. (However, if we can believe magazine and television commercials, the main sprays to dispel the dangers to any relationship are deodorant sprays!)

It should also be noted here that some of the symptoms cited are indications more of a personal dry rot than a marital dry rot. However, a marriage cannot remain vital when the husband and wife making up that marriage have lost their own vitality.

1. The "morning black cloud" syndrome is one indication of dry rot. As its name implies, this strikes mainly in the morning. It expresses itself in several ways: (*a*) Upon waking, one of your first thoughts is, "Oh, not another day!" This indicates that even the turning of the days, the alternation between day and night, has become a burden. (*b*) Upon waking, one has a strong case of the "I don't want to do's." Life itself has become such a burden that one can hardly muster the energy to pursue the necessary responsibilities of the day. Life has become tasteless. (*c*) The "morning black cloud" syndrome expresses itself by a person waking feeling about as fatigued as upon retiring the night before. This is because one is experiencing emotional fatigue rather than physical fatigue. (Of course, one who consistently awakens tired should check with his personal physician.)

2. A second indication of marital dry rot is the need to have some mediating agent in order to relate comfortably

to the mate. As mentioned earlier, dry rot robs one of the ability to simply enjoy the presence of the mate. Many couples can be quite congenial with each other, can laugh and joke with each other, but only so long as they have others around at a party or as guests in the home. When the guests leave they seem to take with them their hosts' ability to relate meaningfully to each other.

3. Related to the above, but slightly different, is the loss of interest in simply being with the mate. These couples find various ways of avoiding being with each other—long hours at work, more trips than necessary out of town, little verbal interaction, the wife's preoccupation with the children and the house, her involvement in too many community activities, or even watching the late, late television movie. Others need two or three drinks before they can enjoy each other.

Perhaps we might get at the point that is being made here if you men ask yourselves honestly, "How would I like to be marooned on a deserted, tropical isle with my wife?" And you wives, "How would I like to be shipwrecked on Robinson Crusoe's island with no one but my husband?"

4. Your marriage is suffering from the dry rot if you have ceased to enjoy the touch of your mate and the stolen glances that communicate a private language between the two of you. Is your first impulse to pull back when your mate touches you, or is your impulse to prolong the touch? Most couples can remember the time when the squeeze of a hand spoke volumes and a stolen glance generated a feeling of warmth for the other. Dry rot dries up such wells of love.

5. Finally, your marriage is suffering from the dry rot when you find yourself continuing to toy with the idea of

being married to someone else. This does not mean that the thought of being married to another never occurs to you. Rather, it means that the idea has become something of a preoccupation that continues to dwell in your mind. Perhaps it is accompanied with fantasies about what marriage would be like with a new mate. A person may even have considered how to get out of the present marriage, and who would take the children. In any case, such fantasies are clear evidence that marital dry rot has infected the marriage.

SOME GUIDELINES FOR AVOIDING MARITAL DRY ROT

It is important that a couple recognize that the dry rot can and will attack their marriage. And dry rot, like other problems, is best dealt with before it has had time to sink its corrosive roots deep into the relationship. The suggestions that follow are not new or profound. However, it has been my observation that certain relatively simple steps taken early in marital difficulties can have a far-reaching effect. Neglected, these difficulties may grow to defy even the most skillful professional help. A minister friend of mine, Joel Land, said sometime ago that marriages may be made in heaven, but the upkeep must be done on earth. In this section we are concerned with that upkeep.

√ 1. *Stay green above the ears.* Two thousand years ago Cicero said there were six mistakes that men in his day made. Among these was the failure to cultivate the mind. Were Cicero to return, he would find us making the same mistake. (This suggests a seventh mistake, namely, the failure to learn from the past mistakes of others.)

Staying green above the ears means remaining mentally

alert, alive, and aware of what is taking place in the world. As stated earlier, a marriage can be no more dynamic and vital than are the people in that relationship. Some marriages die simply because the men and women in them died first. There are many who seem to have stopped thinking about the time they graduated from high school, and have not read anything more profound than a romance magazine during the intervening years. Under these circumstances it is little wonder that this type of person has become a rather shallow, dull husband or wife.

It is probably more difficult for the wife to remain green above the ears than the husband. His work often forces him to come in contact with different ideas and interesting people. But the wife with small children is likely to become so engrossed in her children's lives that she neglects her own personal growth. Her reading runs toward "Humpty-Dumpty" and "Jack and the Beanstalk." When I asked the mother of small children about a particular movie, she said she had not seen it. "In fact," she continued, "I haven't seen anything but Walt Disney movies with the kids for the last five years!"

One of the best ways to stay green above the ears is to read, read, read. Read anything, but read! One needs to read different types of literature, including publications for teen-agers. A parent needs to know what his children are being exposed to. Conferences, lectures, and "meaty" television programs can all help to keep one green above the ears.

2. *Be a friend to yourself.* A friend is someone who knows both our strengths and limitations; he does not reject us because of our limitations and he admires us for our strengths. Some people do not feel that way about themselves. Instead they are filled with feelings of self-criticism,

self-contempt, and self-rejection. Such a person does not make a very exciting mate, nor contribute much toward building a vital marriage. A person with such a low sense of self-esteem cannot provide much emotional support in a marriage; he is too busy beating himself over the head.

Some Christians seem to feel that there is something singularly righteous about constantly berating themselves and depreciating whatever strengths they might have. Yet Jesus admonished us to love our neighbor *as we love ourselves* (Luke 10:27). One of the problems many persons have in loving their neighbor is that of being filled with self-rejection. And those who tend to be highly rejecting of others also show up as highly self-rejecting on psychological tests. (Of course, it is sometimes forgotten that Jesus indicates that loving our neighbor as ourself is preceded by a love for God.)

3. *Make time to be together.* Since time was discussed in the previous chapter, suffice it to say here that love requires time. A marriage cannot be kept vital on an anemic diet of a fleeting moment here and a crumb of time there. Couples who do not *make* time usually do not have time together.

While it is important to have time with the children, it is also important for a husband and wife to get away from the children occasionally. And they need a vacation from *you!* Also, so long as a man and woman are around their children, they may tend to respond as mother and father. But when away from the children, they have a better opportunity to relate to each other as husband and wife.

4. *Make money available for doing things together.* Couples who do not *make* money available for being able to do some things together may very well end up spending it anyway on a marriage counselor or on divorce.

Couples often complain that they have such limited finances they cannot afford an evening out. When a married graduate student tells me that, I often ask, "Could you spare two dollars?" Yes, most any of them can spare that. "Then," I say, "you can have a great night on the town for that price." I then suggest they work out a baby-sitting swap with friends and go to a nice local restaurant where they can get a stack of pancakes at any hour for sixty cents and a cup of coffee for another fifteen. Then they can sit there and leisurely eat and talk with each other. If they sit there long enough, they will be served three cups of coffee! They leave a twenty-five-cent tip and spend the remaining twenty-five cents for a big bag of popcorn at a nearby "discount" store where they can look and plan to their hearts' content about what they are going to buy once he gets out of school. They can then go home somewhat refreshed and with only two dollars gone from their pockets!

Another couple I know have on occasion taken a pound of ground beef which he grills as two large patties at night after the children have gone to bed. The wife puts a loaf of French bread in the oven and makes a tossed salad while the meat grills. Then by candlelight they eat this, along with copious amounts of coffee at a low table in the living room while sitting on pillows. They report that it is very romantic—and costs little too!

Beyond the matter of money, we need to remind ourselves that "the best things in life are free." Though somewhat trite, this statement has much truth in it. These "best things" are closely tied up with the word "relationship." Being together, talking with each other, touching each other, laughing with each other, dreaming with each other —these are all free. If a person does not basically enjoy that kind of relationship with the mate, then a pay raise from the boss will not settle whatever basic problems the dry rot is creating in the marriage.

✓   5. *Keep your affectional life alive.* This reminds me of a cartoon depicting a man and woman sitting in a car under a full moon. He turns to her and says, "Gosh, what a big, beautiful moon; too bad we're married!" The cartoon is humorous because there is truth in it—couples do tend to let their affectional life erode once they are married.

Affection is expressed in many ways—through gifts, a squeeze of the hand, a kiss, a hug, sex, an extraspecial meal, and through verbal expressions of love. With the passing of the months and years, couples often tend to let these small demonstrations of love go unexpressed.

One problem that couples often have in this area is that of understanding the language of love spoken by the partner. One wants to be told he is loved, while the other feels that going about one's daily work is expression enough of love. One wife complained that her husband never came up to hug and kiss her on his own initiative. When asked about this, he responded, "Sure I love her, but I don't see any need to be gooey about it!"

Another concern of couples is a differing need for touching. Basically husbands and wives seem to be either "touch me's" or "touch me not's." "Touch me's" can always sleep better if they have at least a big toe touching the mate. But the "touch me not's" may feel smothered by that big toe.

The important thing here is that each couple must arrive at mutually satisfying ways of expressing their affection to each other. The degree of need for this will vary from couple to couple, but some is needed by all couples if the dry rot is to be avoided.

✓   6. *Remember: Looks aren't everything, but . . .*

Looks may be superficial, but in our society this superficiality does count for something. "Looks are only skin deep," runs an old saying, but this is about as deep as many of us see. There is a tendency for both men and women to let their appearance slide after marriage. The men typically develop a paunch, while their wives grow broader and broader. Wives who are not employed outside the home and therefore have no particular need for dressing well may have more difficulty maintaining their looks than wives who are employed. Nonetheless, counselors often get the impression that one factor in marital dry rot is the loss of interest in one's looks. Consequently, the "other woman" often is trimmer and dresses with more taste than the wife, though she may not be basically more attractive.

7. *Keep the telephone lines open.* Marital dry rot can be combated by a couple if they can communicate verbally in an open and emotionally honest way. If one or the other can say, "Honey, it seems to me that we have drifted apart lately, and I feel a need for putting new life into our marriage," then they have the basis on which to begin working toward revitalizing their relationship. Without this open telephone line, each can only guess at what the other is thinking and feeling. (Marital communication was dealt with more fully in Chapter 2.)

Marital dry rot is much like the common cold—it is seldom fatal, but often incapacitating. Untreated, the cold may develop into pneumonia, and that can be fatal. Unattended, the dry rot can develop into more serious difficulties, leading to divorce. And like the cold that we all occasionally catch, all marriages are subject to "catching" the dry rot.

Chapter 7

THE TOUGH JOB
OF BEING A GOOD PARENT

Middle-class American parents are obsessed with being good parents. Few values rate higher than being Good Mother or Good Father. But American parents are not at all certain that they are succeeding as good parents. So they are anxious. This has led Max Lerner to say, "It is evident that in no other culture has there been so pervasive a cultural anxiety about the rearing of children." (*America as a Civilization,* p. 562.) (I have devoted a chapter to the anxious parent in my book *What's Happening to Our Families?*)

Women in particular have the desire to be good parents. A woman can live reasonably well with a sense of failure as a housekeeper, cook, or lover. But to feel that she has failed as a mother leaves her with an overpowering sense of failure. It is as if she had failed at the very core of her reason for existing.

Perhaps it is from this desire to be a good parent that children are second only to money as a source of quarrels between husband and wives. In fact, even after children are grown and no longer in the home they account for 10 percent of the quarrels. (Blood and Wolfe, *Husbands and Wives: The Dynamics of Married Living,* p. 247.)

It has probably never been easy to be a good parent.

Ancient records document this. One can easily imagine a harried Eve meeting a tired Adam at the door as he returns from the fields. In exasperation and despair she says, "I must be failing someplace; Cain and Abel fight constantly!"

Regardless of the difficulties confronted by earlier generations of parents, this author believes that it is, in fact, more difficult to perform well one's parental role in twentieth-century America than it was in earlier centuries. Numerous factors seem to have conspired to leave the modern parent with a gnawing sense of frustration, failure, and guilt. This chapter will explore some of the reasons for this phenomenon. (An excellent treatment of the subject of parenthood is to be found in E. E. LeMasters, *Parents in Modern America,* and as will be indicated, this writer is indebted to him for some of the ideas expressed herein.)

Dilemmas of the Modern Parent

The contemporary parent is caught between the desire to be a good parent, on the one hand, and several forces that have combined to mitigate against the achievement of that goal, on the other hand.

To begin with, every parent is at the mercy of forces beyond his control in the particular child born into his home. That is, parents have no choice about *which* child is born to them. Often the child's very birth is an "accident." The parents have no control over sex, body build, heredity, or those temperamental qualities which some scientists now think may be genetically determined or influenced. In brief, to become a parent is to commit oneself to a relationship with another human being "sight unseen." One of the facts of life is that parents may have children whom they would not choose as friends. But perhaps the feeling on the part of the child makes it mutual.

Although it does not occur to most of us to quarrel with the fate that placed a particular child in our home, some adults could doubtless be better parents to a different child with a different makeup.

Secondly, being a parent is complicated by the rapid and tumultuous social changes taking place in twentieth-century America. In stable, relatively unchanging societies the matter of being a parent and a child remains rather unchanged from generation to generation. In these societies most all parents rear their children very much alike. They have similar limits, expectations, and goals. Compare that with the host of differing styles of life in your community. Not only are the limits, expectations, and goals for your child different from those you grew up under, but they are also likely to be different from those of other parents in your present community—even the next-door neighbor! Thus, the parents of one child have an eleven o'clock deadline for their child to be in from a date, while other parents have the midnight hour, and others one o'clock. And the age at which a child can start dating in one family is as soon as the child is asked, while another family says, "Not until you're fourteen," and another, "Not until you're sixteen."

The present society is changing so rapidly that child-rearing practices that were appropriate for a grade-school son may not be appropriate for a younger son when he too reaches that age. Thus, the modern parent is deprived of some of the learning experience to be derived from being a parent to older children.

Thirdly, modern parents are faced with a lack of clear

parental models. There is no clear-cut pattern to follow.
They may know more about what parents *were* than what
they *are*. They may know more about what they *don't*
want to be as parents than what they *do* want to be. The
modern father, for example, is faced with a confused
model of a father that is partly derived from the image of
a father in a patriarchal society and partly from the con-
glomerate styles of family life to be found around him today. Part of this model calls for him to be a strong, "head
of the house," authoritarian type of father. Another part
calls for him to be understanding, a friend, confidant, or
even a pal to his children. One model calls for him to be
strict and firm; another calls for freedom and permissiveness. No wonder he is confused! What we need is a clear
model of what it means to be a Good Father or a Good
Mother in this last half of the twentieth century.

Fourthly, the parent's task is made difficult by the decline in parental authority and control. This is especially
true of the father. When Ogburn and Nimkoff some years
ago asked eighteen leading experts on the family to list
some of the most important changes affecting the family
"in recent times," the third most frequent change noted
was the decline in the authority of the husband and father.
(*Technology and the Changing Family,* p. 7.)

Much of the modern child's time is spent away from the
family home in school, entertainment activities, and friend-
ships where the parents have little or no knowledge about
what is happening and consequently little control over the
child's behavior. As LeMasters observes, modern parents
are put in "the unenviable position of having complete responsibility for their offspring but only partial authority
over them." (*Parents in Modern America,* p. 51.) No businessman would accept full responsibility for a task without

being given control over factors influencing the success of that task. But this is exactly the position of that business-man as a parent at home.

Fifthly, the modern parent measures himself with a long yardstick—one with at least forty inches instead of the usual thirty-six! That is, the present generation of parents are not content with being as good as their parents were. They have to be better! They have higher expectations of themselves than their parents had of themselves. If the parents are high school graduates, they want their children to be college graduates. If the father had to work his way through college, he does not want his son to "work like I had to work." Furthermore, in the realm of personal be-havior the parents seem to have higher expectations of themselves. Parents of an earlier generation were likely to attribute Johnny's behavioral problems to a phase he was in, something he learned from bad company, or perhaps to some hereditary cause: "It's that Stevens' blood in him." The modern parent is denied such luxuries. Instead, he blames himself with, "Maybe I'm putting too much pres-sure on him," or other such self-blame explana-tions.

This brings us to a sixth dimension of the problem of being a good parent today—the accusing finger of family experts. When Johnny develops some problem, the modern parent feels himself surrounded by a host of accusing fingers attached to the hands of "experts" who tell him that *he* is to blame for the problem. There are no failures as children, only failures as parents. Most of what the parent reads is likely to remind him that the child is merely a re-flection of the quality of parenting he has received. Conse-quently, rather than help the parent to feel comfortable and confident in his role as parent, the experts often contribute to undermining the parent's self-confidence and create unnecessary anxieties.

Finally, the modern parent's task is complicated by the longer years of dependency of the child. It is commonly recognized that the human offspring is dependent upon his parents for many more years than any other living creature. What is not recognized sometimes is that these years of dependency are increasing. This is particularly true in those families in which a college education is considered important. Not only is the parent responsible for seeing that the child gets a high school education, but he must now continue his responsibility on through college and perhaps graduate school. College and graduate school are considered a child's *right* in some circles. Even marriage may not free the parent of this financial responsibility. Many parents continue some support to their college-enrolled children after marriage. While there are still those who believe that, "If you're old enough to get married, you're old enough to support yourself," their tribe is diminishing. To be sure, many parents welcome these extended years of dependency, since it contributes to a continued feeling of being needed.

All the above factors combine to make the modern parent's role a difficult one. As with marriage, he is stuck with his role as parent "for better or worse." But unlike marriage, there is no provision made in the society for "resigning." We do have a societally approved method for withdrawing from marriage—divorce. Fortunately, most of us have no desire to resign as parents. But probably there are days when any parent would like to resign for a few hours.

THE MYTHS OF PARENTHOOD

Parenthood today is difficult, partly because of the host of myths that surround the subject of children. Consequently, some of the realities of parenthood are glossed over. "Myth" as used here refers to a widely held belief in the society which has enough truth in it to make it credible but which is largely ungrounded in fact. Such myths tend to select one aspect of reality, lift it out of context, and then romanticize that small aspect of reality.

There is a need to sort out reality from fantasy in the family. To this end, there has been a growing interest in recent years in the mythology surrounding family life. Richard Udry deals with some of these myths in his book *The Social Context of Marriage* (Chapter 11). But the best treatment of the subject as it pertains to parents is provided by LeMasters in *Parents in Modern America*. He lists seventeen items of what he calls the "folklore" of parenthood. Among the folk beliefs listed by him are:

1. *Children improve a marriage*. While it is true that couples with children have significantly lower divorce rates, perhaps twice as low, LeMasters is correct in stating that this is not the same as *improving* a marriage (p. 28). One of the more common statements made to me as a marriage counselor by unhappily married couples is, "If it hadn't been for the children, I would have gotten out of this a long time ago." So the lower divorce rate among couples with children may simply reflect the reluctance to abandon a marriage in which children are present. In this case it says nothing about the *quality* of the relationship between the parents.

Although it is doubtless true that there are many marriages which are enhanced by the presence of children, there is mounting evidence that the birth of children into a home may destroy some marriages. Reuben Hill has said, "We must face up to the fact that more and more our research suggests that the advent of a child is not necessarily the fulfillment of marriage but possibly the first point of cleavage that separates husband and wife." ("The Most Unexpected Threat to a Good Marriage," *McCall's,* July, 1967, pp. 94 ff.) This is further supported by the research of Harold Feldman, who studied the various stages of the marriage cycle. Dr. Feldman found that the most familiar pattern of marital satisfaction is U-shaped. ("Marital Satisfaction Over the Family Life Cycle," *Journal of Marriage and the Family,* February, 1970, pp. 20–28.) That is, satisfaction is highest early in the marriage before children arrive or when they are quite young, and late in the marriage after the children are gone. It is lowest during the child-rearing years and continues to decline with the birth of each additional child.

The above suggests that in addition to asking, "What do parents do to children?" we must now also ask, "What do children do to marriage?" Generally, I suspect that children make a marriage a little more of what it already is. That is, if the couple basically has a good relationship, then the birth of a child will enhance that relationship. But if the couple is basically unhappy with each other, then, rather than cementing their relationship, a child will only serve to make them more unhappy.

2. *Child-rearing is fun.* Not only does folklore say that a child cements a marriage together, but an idea is also afoot that being a parent is great *fun.* This idea is perhaps encouraged by at least two factors. The first is the baby itself. Anything as cute as "that little doll" would just have

to be fun. Also, note how often people remark, "How little; how helpless." Perhaps they feel it would be fun to have such a cute, helpless little thing around the house. Secondly, I suspect that grandmothers themselves help perpetuate this idea. Their selective memories recall mainly the pleasant parts of parenthood and not those days when they would gladly have resigned as a mother, if they only could.

To be sure, being a parent is rewarding, meaningful, fulfilling, exciting, challenging. But I suspect that few of us are ready to attach the term "fun" to parenthood. It is work. Writing this book is exciting and challenging, but I could by no stretch of the imagination call it fun. It is among the hardest work I do. So is being a parent.

Once while addressing a group of women, I raised the question, in a somewhat rhetorical way, as to why anyone in his right mind would want a child. I then went on to ask what would happen if someone offered a family a pet that could be described as physically painful to acquire, very expensive over a period of twenty years to keep, noisy, smelly, disorganized, emotionally draining, time-consuming, nerve-racking, expressing little appreciation for what is done for it, and in the end may break the family's heart? Yet this is one description of a child. At that point I was interrupted by an angry woman in her fifties and was accused of being antichild. On other occasions a few women have objected to such a description of a child. Interestingly, they have all been women whose children have long since left home. Young mothers of preschool children, in particular, find it an apt description. Have the older women forgotten the tedious details of being a mother?

The point being made is that it is a myth to think of child-rearing as fun. This is not to say that some of our deepest joys and most fulfilling rewards don't come from being a part of our children's lives and helping them to grow into adulthood. Very few of us would want to "send our children back"—but parenthood isn't *fun*.

3. *Children will turn out well if they have "good" parents*. This bit of folklore is related to another that says: There are no bad children, only bad parents. While these generalizations are probably basically true, they fail to take into account all the other factors that impinge on a child's life. This myth, if believed by the parent, forces him into the untenable position of assuming *full* responsibility for every personality quirk, every behavioral problem, every adjustmental hang-up experienced by the child. It fails to take cognizance of the tremendous role of one's peer group, the schools, the mass media, the world political climate, and one's heredity in the shaping of a personality. Almost everyone can name at least one family in which all the children in the family turned out well except the one "black sheep." How do we account for this "black sheep"? To be sure, no two siblings grow up in identically the same home, but to lay the full blame at the door of the parents for one child turning out bad after they have done so well with the other children hardly makes sense to some of us. (And if we are to blame them for the "black sheep," we must also give them full credit for the others who turned out well.)

All of this reminds us that in the role of parent, there is a slender margin of error granted. (LeMasters, *Parents in Modern America,* p. 60.) We can accept philosophically the fact that not all marriages will work. We expect some divorces. But the parent who rears one or more children who grow up to be responsible, contributing members of society, and then has one "black sheep," may be remembered mainly for the "black sheep."

4. *Today's parents are not as good as those of yesterday.* Americans tend to romanticize the past. Consequently, "old-fashioned religion," "old-fashioned love," "old-fashioned cooking," and even "old-fashioned parents" are somehow conceived of as being better than those of the present. Anyone who reads history, biographies, and autobiographies knows that parents of the past have not always been so outstanding. Some child-rearing practices of the past would make many modern parents' blood run cold. An 1834 issue of *Mother's Magazine* emphasizes the importance of breaking a child's will. It cites with approval a parent whose young daughter refused to say "dear momma" and was whipped off and on for four hours before being forced into compliance! Once children were whipped into such submission, the author reported, they seldom gave much more trouble. (Margaret Mead and Martha Wolfenstein, eds., *Childhood in Contemporary Cultures,* p. 160.)

If our forefathers were better parents, it is only because they did not have to cope with a highly industrialized, complex, urbanized society such as that in which the modern parent is forced to rear children. Given similar circumstances, they would have done as well—or as poorly —as present-day parents.

5. *Love is all you need to be a good parent.* Americans have an unfailing and unshakable faith in love. The twin myth to this is, "All we need to get married on is love." Just as love is not enough to get married on (nearly 100 percent of those getting divorced were in love at one time), even so, love is not all it takes to be a good parent. Twenty years ago Bruno Bettelheim wrote a book, *Love Is Not Enough,* the thesis of which was that feelings

of warmth and affection—love—must be tempered and guided by knowledge, understanding, and self-control on the part of the parent. The intervening years have not changed that fact.

This is not to diminish the importance of love. It is to say that the myth which says that love is all there is to being a good parent has told only half of the truth.

6. *Behavioral science has been helpful to parents.* LeMasters asserts that psychology, psychiatry, sociology, and other related fields have largely based their pronouncements about parenthood on flimsy research. They have often made assumptions about the bases of human behavior that are poorly supported by solid research, and the sum result has been to contribute to feelings of guilt, anxiety, and inadequacy on the part of the parent. (*Parents in Modern America,* pp. 32–49.)

This myth about the value of behavioral sciences for parents is similar to other myths in that it has enough truth in it to be dangerous. Perhaps the most damaging result of a blind faith in behavioral sciences is that it has contributed to undermining parents' self-confidence and ability to think creatively about their own problems. Consequently, they have become so "expert oriented" that they dare not take any initiative with their own child without expert approval.

Beyond a doubt, the behavioral sciences have been of help in understanding human behavior. In the hands of competent specialists, who know the limitations of their speciality, behavioral sciences will continue to offer hope of helping people with their problems. But it must always be remembered that the research usually cited by naïve authors of popular magazine articles is always concerned with generalities and never with specific individuals. As stated in my book *What's Happening to Our Families?* (p. 92), modern parents do well to read the books by experts, listen to their lectures, read their articles, but then *in the light of this knowledge, plus the knowledge of their own particular child, follow their own better sense of judgment.* And that applies to this book as well!

Having looked at some reasons why modern parents have a difficult task being good parents, let us now turn to the more positive side of the subject and discuss some guidelines toward being less anxious as a parent.

TOWARD BEING LESS ANXIOUS AS A PARENT

Parents ought to be anxious when they have not measured up to their own better sense of judgment. In this case, anxiety may constructively motivate them to change. However, modern parents are often unnecessarily anxious. This kind of anxiety, rather than bringing out the best in them, tends to paralyze their ability to deal creatively with their role as parents. I believe that the recognition and acceptance of certain basic facts regarding our children will help allay some unnecessary anxieties. Let us briefly examine these:

1. *Parents are not the only influence shaping their child's life.* A multitude of forces combine in a thousand ways to mold the personality and values of our children. Among these are at least twelve years of school, an estimated twenty thousand hours of television by age eighteen, hundreds of movies, thousands of hours of music on the radio, a dozen youth organizations, scores of fads, countless political issues, and endless world tensions. In addition, one must include the child's biological drives and hereditary

traits which influence personality but about which little is presently known.

We have also doubtless underestimated the profound impact of the peer group in shaping the values of children. Too often parental values wither in the face of peer pressures. As David Riesman observes in *The Lonely Crowd:* "There has been an enormous ideological shift favoring submission to the group. . . . The peer group becomes the measure of all things; the individual has few defenses the group cannot batter down" (p. 82).

We must also recognize that the values espoused and projected by most of the mass media are probably in conflict with those of many homes. Take time to examine the values underlying the movies, television, radio, and reading materials to which children are exposed. These media will be found to emphasize sexual permissiveness, impulse gratification, violence, the pursuit of pleasure, living for today, crass materialism, the worship of the immaturities of youth, and easy success. These are hardly values that most parents would hope to inculcate in their children.

2. *A child's psyche is rather durable.* Some psychologists believe that one has to do rather consistently the wrong thing at the wrong time over a period of years in order to seriously damage a child's psychological development. This is to say that parents who become anxious as to whether they have warped their child's personality because of some particular mistake probably can rest at ease. Although there are single events that can have a lifelong negative impact, these are usually of a very traumatic nature. Also, closer examination will reveal other circumstances in the person's life that combined to make the experience traumatic.

This writer recalls engaging in a discussion with his wife

prior to the birth of their first child. I said that we would need to be careful so as not to break the child's spirit and will. That concern has long since been forgotten! That child, a son now fourteen, quickly dispelled any thoughts about the fragility of his will. We have sometimes found ourselves fighting to keep our own wills from being shattered by that child! This has been equally true with our daughter.

3. *You will not be an ideal parent.* You will not be an ideal parent because you are not living in an ideal society, nor in an ideal world, nor do you have an ideal child, nor are you an ideal person. These are facts! The writer regularly has students in one of his classes write autobiographical papers. Having read hundreds of these papers over the years, he has reached one conclusion: Regardless of how well parents do as parents, they are going to fall short in some ways in the estimation of their children. He recalls the daughter of a physician who could find nothing wrong with the way her parents had reared her, nothing. Then she concluded her paper by saying that they had been too perfect; that she would have learned more about life had they not been so perfect! Sometimes you cannot win.

Another conclusion has been reached from reading these autobiographical papers—that in spite of their failures as parents, children still love those parents who express even a modicum of affection for and interest in their children.

4. *If you are a good parent, your child will not always feel warm toward you.* Parents who feel a need to have the constant approval and warm affection of their children are in for trouble. A parent must at times make unpopular decisions. The child will respond in anger. Since some parents cannot tolerate such anger, they "buy" the approval of the child by acquiescing. However, if this is done over a

period of time, perhaps years, they are certain to lose the child's respect. Unwittingly the parents allow themselves to be manipulated by the child's anger. With some adults, the accusation from the child of being a poor parent is enough to wither the wisest parental decision. The parent-child relationship can survive without constant feelings of warmth; it cannot remain vital without mutual respect.

In concluding this chapter, I might note that in spite of the differences of opinion among child-rearing specialists, there is a rather common agreement that despite whatever differences in styles of life might exist from family to family, effective parents usually possess certain basic qualities. Among these are: (*a*) *An ability to accept the child warmly*. Without this the child is thwarted in being able to love healthily and to perceive himself to be a worthwhile person. (*b*) *Consistent parenting behavior*. That is, the way the parent relates to the child is consistent from day to day. Some parents seem to love the child to death one hour and hate him the next. A child from a consistently harsh home is possibly better off than one in which the parent vacillates between love and rejection. (*c*) *The establishment of clear limits of behavior*. The particular limits will vary from family to family. It is important that they be clearly understood by the child and consistently enforced by the parent. Without limits, the child becomes confused and anxious. Without learning to live within limits at home, the child will have difficulty living within the reality limits once he moves into the outside world.

Chapter 8

THE GENERATION GAP: WHAT'S IT ALL ABOUT?

Generation gap! The term strikes a reaction in almost everyone, young and old. It has become a major preoccupation of Americans. A recent Gallup Poll found that one expression of the generation gap, campus unrest, is considered by the public to be the major problem confronting Americans. (The Gallup Poll, June 18, 1970.)

Interestingly, there is some question as to whether there is, in fact, a generation gap at all. One point of view holds that what we call a generation gap is nothing new but simply the friction that has existed between parents and children of every previous generation. The other point of view holds that instead of a generation *gap,* what we have is a vast and yawning generation *chasm.* The world in which the older generation grew up has changed to such a radical degree that it might be said to exist no longer. This leads Margaret Mead to assert that the only true natives in our present society are the young, and that it is we, the older generation, who are the immigrants. (*Culture and Commitment: A Study of the Generation Gap,* pp. 72–78.) It is out of this native-immigrant situation that the generation gap is born.

It is the purpose of this chapter to explore this gap (or chasm), to try to understand what the new generation is like, and what this has to do with ordinary families and their children in the '70s.

For most ordinary families today, there will likely be no radical changes in the values, ideals, and styles of life between the parents and children in the next decade. There is reason to believe that most young people, whether they go on to college or not, continue to accept the basic values of the parents. They will probably finish their education, take a job, work for advancement, marry, buy a home, and have children much as their parents have done. Nonetheless, subtle changes have been and will continue to take place even in these young adults. For instance, they are not willing to wait ten years for a new home and new furniture, as did their parents. They want it now. This is the "now" generation, and they will get the home and furniture now.

In other families, however, there is, or will be, a growing chasm between the parents and the children insofar as their values, ideals, and styles of life are concerned. This younger group tends to scorn the importance of hard work, "getting ahead," independence, religion, and the traditional codes of sexual behavior—ideals highly valued by the parents. However, it is the opinion of most authorities that the attitudes, values, and behavior of this group should be watched, since they are expected to become the predominant pattern among young people in the '70s, '80s, and '90s. If this be so, it behooves present-day parents to try to understand the strange, irritating, rebellious behavior of this group, since the child now in the cradle may become much more like them than unlike them. Conseqently, much of this chapter focuses on this small but influential minority.

THE WORLDS OF THE OLD AND YOUNG GENERATIONS

It will be of help in understanding the generation gap if we pause first to take a brief look at the worlds in which the older and gounger generations have grown up and are growing up.

Parents of the present young generation grew up in the economically deprived years of the Great Depression and World War II. A great debate raged during the late '30s as to whether or not the United States should get involved in the European war. Isolationists said we should stay out. After all, a vast ocean separated us from that far-off conflict. World War II changed all that. The advent of jet flight, rockets, and a worldwide communications network has today shrunk that ocean into a small fishing lake only minutes from shore to shore.

To that generation, the life goals were to establish "peace and prosperity" (a slogan of the day) and to make money to purchase all the consumer goods that they had been deprived of in their youth. Products of the nation's shops and factories became the sought-after "Promised Land"; education and hard work were Moses and Joshua leading them into that paradise; but some feared that they might not make it, since those were also the years of the cold war when the "Philistines" (Communists) were viewed as threatening to take over from either without or within the country. It was this fear that gave rise to Senator Joe McCarthy and his Communist hunts. Of course, many people reached the "Promised Land"; and for more than twenty-five years now an older generation of white middle-class Americans has drunk deeply of the milk and honey of an affluent society. But they always remember the "seven lean years" of their youth.

Contrast that world with the present one in which young people find themselves. Where poverty of the depression shaped the lives of their parents, this new generation has grown up knowing nothing but affluence. They take it for granted. And with the growing use of computers in factories, all predictions are for a continued growing standard of living with goods produced by fewer and fewer people.

The fruits of an industrialized society continue to delight the older generation—dishwashers, television, self-cleaning ovens, stereo record players, speed boats. But the young can never remember a time when it was any different. They take these things for granted. The past to them is a far country, across an ocean of time. Furthermore, many of the younger generation do not share this enthusiasm with the progress of industrialization. As one young person said: "How can you call it progress? You have made the air unbreathable, the polluted streams kill the fish, our natural resources are being dissipated, autos clog the streets and countryside, the milk we drink contains strontium 90, and our vegetables reek of pesticides. But you call it progress!"

About the time the new generation was born, the world was abruptly and dramatically thrust into the electronic age. Today the whole world is caught in an interlocking network of electronic communications. What was an ocean barrier to one generation is so insignificant as scarcely to merit attention to the present electronic age. This generation has grown up with almost instant reporting of events from the far corners of the world. Because of this, particularly television, they are no longer ignorant about how others live, and they no longer feel remote, untouched by events on the other side of the world. Whereas their parents considered themselves citizens of a nation, their children in many respects consider themselves to be world citizens.

Many of the younger generation have become sensitized to the subtle (and sometimes not so subtle) hypocrisies of our society. They score the older generation for its schizophrenic living, for talking of equality but squelching those who seek to claim it, for talking of love but practicing indifference, for panicking when they have lost their jobs but proudly proclaiming that if the poor weren't so lazy, they could find work. It is not enough for the older generation to say, "But look how much things have improved since I was a child." Nor is it enough to say, "You've told me about my hypocrisies, now tell me about yours." Nor will bumper stickers proclaiming, "America, love it or leave it" get the job done. All that the young know is that the "words of our mouths and the meditations of our hearts" do not coincide. They should.

In brief, the forces that have shaped the worlds of parents and children are vastly different. The parents' lives were shaped by two world wars, economic boom and bust, hunger, poverty, the decay of rural America, the radio, and the automobile. The new generation's lives have been shaped by prosperity, worldwide television, the bomb, jet flight, the growth and decay of our sprawling cities, freewheeling technology, and the destruction of our natural environment. Because of this, Margaret Mead says that until recently our elders could say, "I have been young and you have never been old." But today the young can reply, "You have never been young in the world I am young in." (*Culture and Commitment: A Study of the Generation Gap,* p. 63.) Herein lies the generation gap—

two worlds. And because of this, neither generation can really understand the other. Each is left in its loneliness, neither one able to experience the world of the other.

THE NEW GENERATION: WHAT IS IT LIKE?

In this section we will attempt to develop some under-standing of what the emerging new generation is like. It should be understood that the characteristics set forth here will not be applicable to most of the present generation. Rather, *our* purpose is to capture the trend of the *future*. One way of trying to predict the future shape of things is by studying certain "trend setters," sometimes called the *avant-garde*. The Beatles, for instance, were the *avant-garde* at one time. One might at that time have predicted by observation something of the dress and hair styles that would later become popular. Now, dress styles, haircuts, and glasses once considered outrageous as worn by the Beatles have become popular and accepted by the man on the street. Even staid businessmen now wear their hair and sideburns much longer—something once found only on the *avant-garde*. (Of course, it is not always easy to determine who the *avant-garde* are.)

Now, what is the young generation like and in what di-rection might our children be moving in this decade of the '70s? A study commissioned by *Fortune* magazine and reported in the January, 1969, issue is pertinent to this question. This study explored some of the attitudes and ideas of the current college and noncollege young adults eighteen to twenty-four years of age. About one out of every nine Americans falls into this age category.

The *Fortune* study focused primarily on the college

group. About three out of five fell into what they call the "practical-minded" students. These see college primarily as a means of "bettering" themselves, of getting a better job with increasing income. By contrast, about two out of five college students, called "forerunners," tend to take college for granted. One just naturally goes to college. They do not see college as a way of making more money. Most of them come from affluent families and they take affluence for granted. Their reasons for being in college are not clearly defined, but they generally see it as a way for "changing things."

Fortune termed this latter group "forerunners," because they (along with many sociologists and psychologists) believe that their attitudes about going to college, making money, careers, affluence, politics, etc., will become increasingly characteristic of young people and the society in the future. It should be stressed that forerunners should not be thought of only as radicals and hippies. Most of them could not be detected by their dress or speech. Many of them are from the ordinary families with whom this book is concerned. Also, the discussion that follows below should not be thought of as describing only hippies and radicals. Some of these qualities will describe the children of adult readers of this book.

Back to the question asked earlier: What is the emerging new generation like? What ideas, values, and behavior characterize them?

1. The outstanding feature of the emerging generation is their *challenge and rejection of many of the most deeply held American values.* Among these values are the importance of hard work, of knowledge, of "getting ahead," of patriotism, of respect for authority, of the church, of the democratic process, of traditional sex ethics, of the

scientific process, of the primacy of property rights. Many of the new generation have lost faith in the American judicial system, political and religious leaders, America as "the land of the free and the home of the brave," and in science which is said to bring us better things for better living.

The *Fortune* study revealed that about half of the forerunners indicate that they have less faith in the democratic process than do their parents. About half believe that the United States is a sick society. Two thirds support draft resistance. About half believe it is appropriate to engage in civil disobedience to further causes they support. And almost 10 percent said they would support civil disobedience *no matter what issues were involved!* However, the editor assumes that some do not really mean what they say, since it is difficult to envision them supporting civil disobedience by, say, the Ku-Klux Klan. But it does suggest nihilistic tendencies in the group. (Daniel Seligman, "A Special Kind of Rebellion," *Fortune,* January, 1969, p. 68.) Revolutionaries such as Che Guevara and Stokely Carmichael were admired by this group more than were President Lyndon Johnson or President Richard Nixon (p. 71).

The existence of dissident attitudes revealed by the *Fortune* report are not surprising. These have been known to be held by student activists. What is surprising, the editor says, is that such a large percentage of nonactivist students share similar ideas. It would appear, then, that behind the small and highly visible activist minority is a larger, "silent" group who share similar dissident attitudes (p. 68).

The challenging of cherished values is not to be utterly decried. The values of a society need to be reexamined by each new generation in the light of new circumstances. Some may need rejection. What is disturbing to many is that this generation seems to reject deeply held values without examination, and sometimes simply because they are held by the society as a whole, the Establishment.

2. The emerging generation is *anti-institution and anti-authority*. Traditional institutions and authorities are widely distrusted and often detested. The anti-institutional sentiments of the young are excellently summed up by Ernest Campbell, who says, "They want love but not marriage, religious experience but not church, learning but not schools, citizenship but not government." (*Christian Manifesto,* p. 80.) Institutions of the society are seen either as irrevelant relics of the past or as tools of the Establishment to curb and impinge upon the freedom of the new generation.

This anti-Establishment attitude is perhaps best seen in the religious realm. Hordes of the young (not counting many of the older generation) consider themselves religious, some deeply so, but have nothing to do and want nothing to do with institutionalized religion. Within both Protestantism and Catholicism groups have sprung up that operate outside the institutionalized church. These may be as vague and unorganized as the "underground church," or as organized as the Full Gospel Businessmen's Fellowship, Campus Crusade for Christ, Inter-Varsity Fellowship, and the Fellowship of Christian Athletes. These organizations are unspoken criticisms of the institutionalized church, in effect saying that it was not getting the job done. Of course, the history of any movement is that if it survives, it goes through an evolutionary process that includes becoming institutionalized itself. At least one of the above groups is presently rather rigidly controlled from a central national headquarters. So there seems to be no escape from institutions. Also, these groups frequently look to the institutionalized church for financial support and workers.

3. The emerging generation tends to be *anti-intellectual and antirational*. There is an increasing distrust of knowledge and rationality among many of the younger generation. Consequently, there is relatively little interest in books, research, and the usual academic disciplines. This is a radical departure from the past. As Peter Drucker observes: "For the first time since Socrates established knowledge as the fountainhead of Western thought and the Western world-view 2400 years ago, we are coming to question the value of knowledge. Are we to abandon the foundation on which the modern West has been built?" (*The Age of Discontinuity,* p. 370.) He goes on to speculate that perhaps the loss of faith in knowledge is due to the fact that it has often been misused in creating instruments and conditions that are inimical to the welfare of man.

This anti-intellectual, antirational stance is reflected in the changes that sociologist Raymond Rymph, of Purdue University, has observed in the new generation of student:

> I think a student is somebody who looks toward studies . . . ideas, concepts, thoughts, cognitions. A student relates to the cognitive state, but that doesn't happen any more. . . . Today's student is not interested in cognitive states, he's interested in affective states. He wants to feel things. So you say "do you really think its rational to sit in the armory" and they say its unimportant whether its rational or not "the important thing is that I 'feel' that this is what I

ought to do." (*Purdue Exponent,* May 22, 1970, pp. 4–5.)

Many no longer want to start learning with books, they want to begin with experience. This is excellently summed up in a statement about a seminary experiment in ecumenical education. One of those involved, Sister Kathleen Daly, is quoted as saying: "We're reversing the whole process. Instead of starting with books and trying to apply what they say to the world, we're starting with life itself. You might say we're creating truth." (*New York Times,* March 12, 1969.)

Some of the young have withdrawn their faith in traditional academic approaches to knowledge because they have seen the deadening fragmentation that rigid analysis and pure logic sometimes lead to. They have also observed cold rationality's brutal heartlessness. The veneration of modern man as a rational creature has been one of the myths of the twentieth century. The young challenge the rationality of modern man, pointing to the irrational, wanton slaughter of countless millions of human beings since 1900. This "rational" century has witnessed the mass execution of more millions than any other century in history—and it has three decades yet remaining!

The point is, the new generation has lost some faith in traditional intellectual and rational pursuits. Increasingly, they look within their own experience and feelings for guides to behavior. Instead of studying books, many of them are insisting on studying the "original documents"— people themselves. That might not be such a bad idea.

4. Related to the above and yet somewhat different is the *loss of faith in science* as the answer to man's problems. Science fiction movies of the '40s, '50s, and early

'60s usually depicted the world as thrown into chaos by the arrival of some threat. In the midst of this chaos arose the learned scientist (often with a German accent) who, godlike, brought order out of chaos and, through science, saved the world. The demise of such films may be related to a loss of faith in the saving efficacy of omnipotent, omniscient science. As Paul Goodman says, "Science has not produced the general happiness that people expected, and now it has fallen under the sway of greed and power; whatever its beneficent past, people fear that its further progress will do more harm than good." ("Today's Youth," *Chicago Tribune,* September 14, 1969.)

Because the tradition of science and technology has served the West well for three hundred years, Theodore Roszak is surprised that almost overnight and with hardly a debate a significant proportion of the young have "opted out of that tradition." (*The Making of a Counter Culture,* p. 141.)

Instead of viewing science as an all-knowing, all-powerful, and benevolent savior, modern youth are coming to view it as a raging beast, partially harnessed, but now threatening to destroy its master.

5. *The new generation tends to emphasize the present and reject the past.* The "now" generation has little interest in history. But perhaps they do not so much reject the past as ignore it as being irrelevant to their own experience. Daniel Seligman believes that one reason a modern-day son may not respect his father's authority is that he has little reason to view his father's experience as relevant to his own. ("A Special Kind of Rebellion," *Fortune,* January, 1969, p. 174.) He may, in fact, have only a vague idea of what his father really does at work.

Nor does he envision himself following in his father's foot-steps. It is, therefore, unrealistic for the son to suppose that he might be doing the same thing someday. This stands in sharp contrast to those cultures in which the son grows into manhood having learned from his father the skills necessary for life.

Margaret Meads says that in many cultures in which change takes place very, very slowly, a grandparent hold-ing a new grandchild in his arms cannot conceive of any other future for the child than that of his own past life. (*Culture and Commitment: A Study of the Generation Gap,* p. 1.) So the past is very relevant to the present and the future. But in much of the world today, change moves so swiftly that the oldest and the youngest child in the same family grow up in somewhat different worlds. Prob-lems that parents confront with the youngest child, but not with the oldest, may be related to the fact that the younger one is growing up in different circumstances, un-der different pressures, and has different problems with which to cope.

While the older generation might argue about how ir-relevant the past is, we must remind ourselves that much of the past is irrelevant. Most of today's college graduates will be taking *jobs that did not exist when they were born.* And it is estimated that *half of all our present knowledge will be obsolete in ten years!*

This generation's disinterest in history leads Robert Albrook to say, "A new generation never knows what lies ahead; this new generation does not know what lies be-hind." ("One Thing Sure, Parenthood Today Is No Bore," *Fortune,* January, 1969, p. 92.) They are only concerned with now. Having cut themselves off from the past, and being unable to fathom the future, this young generation, sociologist Kenneth Keniston concludes, is *stranded in the present*. ("Stranded in the Present," in Sheldon Garber, ed., *Adolescence for Adults,* p. 74.) Being stranded in the present tends to minimize one's sense of responsibility to the past or the future. So they live for the experiences of the present, whether these be drugs or sex, sometimes with little concern for the implications of their behavior.

7. The emerging generation seems to be *moving from an individual identity to a corporate identity*. That is, individualism may continue to wane in the '70s and young people (as well as the older generation) will seek personal identity in group identity. The Haight-Ashbury scene has largely faded into history. But some sociologists think the hippies there may have pioneered a new style of life (in spirit at least) for the future, a style of life that seeks more involvement in intimate social groups. While it is doubtful that the communes which some of the present young have founded will ever appeal to but a small percentage of the population, the spirit of that type of life, the corporate orientation, may spread.

Paul Goodman sees in the idealism of the new youth a kind of religious faith in which a main sacrament is the powerful workings of the "close presence of other human beings, without competition or one-upping." Then he says, "What a drastic comment on the dehumanization and fragmentation of the modern times that salvation can be attained simply by the 'warmth of assembled animal bodies,' as Kafka called it, describing his mice." ("Today's Youth," *Chicago Tribune,* September 14, 1969.)

This corporate orientation was reflected in the reports of some youths (and faculty) who participated in the November, 1969, March on Washington. The main responses subsequently reported to me by those who attended were:

"Everybody seemed so concerned"; "Everybody asked if you had a place to stay or were hungry"; "We felt that we all belonged together." Similar reports emerge from the various "rock festivals," such as the one at Woodstock. Commenting on this kind of "oneness" or corporate existence, David Maxey said that during the March on Washington and the rally at the foot of the Washington Monument, "food passed from hand to hand like Communion bread. And when the music moved them, the crowd swayed like one organism." ("Mr. President, Bring Us Together Again," *Look,* January 27, 1970, p. 18.)

Marshall McLuhan expects that the years ahead will witness a moving away from a society that values rugged individualism toward one in which cooperation and corporate qualities are valued. In fact, he sees in the new generation's desire to be together, live together, share together a movement toward "retribalization" and the emergence of a "neo-tribal" man. (*Understanding Media.*) That is, just as persons in tribal cultures have little identity apart from the tribe, even so will our society move toward a retribalization in which one's identity will be closely tied to the group (tribe) with which he is identified. If McLuhan is right, and the new generation does herald the shape of life in the future, then neo-tribal people will see themselves more as a part of the larger organism than as individual agents. They will value cooperation more than individual initiative and competition. They will be almost totally involved in the life of the group. Neo-tribal man, McLuhan says, is cast into a "seamless web of interdependence."

Perhaps we already have some expressions of this type of life in the self-contained, close-knit retirement villages that flourished in the '60s. In these villages many activities are shared in common and could become models for a type of more intimate, corporate living in the future.

This may also be reflected in our television entertainment. The rugged individualist of early television, the Lone Ranger, has given way to the Cartwrights of *Bonanza,* whose lives are closely intertwined with each other.

How Shall the Older Generation Respond?

Whatever the older generation has failed to do, it has not failed to respond to this emerging generation. It has responded in *anger* when the young have rejected and scorned its most cherished values. It has responded in *guilt,* wondering whether the behavior of the young reflected their own failure as parents. It has responded in *envy* over the (apparently) carefree and irresponsible lives of the young. It has responded in *jealousy* of the sexual potency of the young men and the uninhibited response of their dates. It has responded with *loneliness,* feeling left out, out of date, out of step; this has led many to attempt to join the ranks of the young. It has responded in *resistance,* for the history of man has been to resist each change. It has responded with *disillusionment.* As a father said who had just found that his eighteen-year-old daughter was on marijuana, "All my life I've been taught that if one worked hard, paid his debts, kept his nose clean, and loved God, then everything would turn out all right; now this has happened!"

A recent popular song admonished us to listen to what the children say. One response the older generation must make is to *listen* to the young (and we would hope this is a two-way street). In the extreme behavior of youth often lies profound truth. (Youth knows no moderation, only extremes.) What might we learn? As noted earlier, the new generation often questions knowledge and science. Face it, knowledge and science have often been prostituted by industrial societies, and through industry we have now "progressed" to the point that we may not much longer be able to breathe our air or drink our water. There must be a lesson in there. Some youth seem to fail to value education highly, especially college. Great! Who says every ambitious young person *ought* to go to college? Some of these bright minds need to go to technical or business schools. The young generation seems more interested in feelings than in knowledge. Perhaps our cold, impersonal society could use some "heart" or "soul." The educated man of the future may be one who is measured not alone by his knowledge but also by his ability to feel, to be sensitive to people.

"Up with People" pins worn by some of the young underline a fact that human need often takes a backseat to the needs of business and industry. (An individual ticketed for creating too much smoke while burning trash has his name printed in the paper. A Louisiana firm recently released enough mercury in its wastes to pollute thousands of dollars of food fish, but its name was withheld!) The lack of interest in "getting ahead," of competing in the business world may not be all bad. The Organization Man tends to sign the title of his soul over to the Organization in exchange for profit.

Already many of the ideas of the young that were once considered extreme and radical are becoming integrated into the society and even accepted by the Establishment. This is best seen when comparing the values of the old

and new cultures (or we might say old and new generations). P. E. Slater summarizes these thus:

> The old culture, when forced to choose, tends to give
> preference to property rights over personal rights,
> technological requirements over human needs, com-
> petition over cooperation, violence over sexuality,
> concentration over distribution, the producer over
> the consumer, means over ends, secrecy over open-
> ness, social reforms over personal expression, striv-
> ing over gratification, oedipal love over communal
> love, and so on. The new counter culture tends to
> reverse all these priorities. ("Cultures in Collision,"
> *Psychology Today,* July, 1970, p. 31.)

In our day we are seeing a reversal of these values
taking place. (Not that the new generation can claim
credit for all these changes.) One young man, Ralph
Nader, has become a "consumer advocate," giving rise to
increasing interest on the part of the Federal Government
in consumer rights. Recent "truth in packaging" laws are
one outcome of this interest. Furthermore, no longer can
industry or government expect to go unchallenged when
either impinges on human need. More than one project
has been stopped when families were being displaced before the bulldozer razed their homes to make room for
yet another monument to an industrial society. But the
accepting of "young ideas" expresses itself in other ways.
Life magazine (June 12, 1970, pp. 50–56) has reported
on Americans who, hippie-like, are "dropping out." These
successful men refuse any longer to play the game of "getting on top." Instead, they have chosen to pursue another
career, where they can "do their own thing."

Margaret Mead says that in the emerging age adults
will learn from the child; they will have to survive in a

world of change. (*Culture and Commitment: A Study of the Generation Gap,* p. 94.) But wasn't it a prophet who long ago predicted a time when "a little child shall lead them"?

I conclude this book on ordinary families at the onset of the '70s. One wonders how much of it will prove to be obsolete a decade from now at the dawning of the '80s. But we can be sure that ordinary families of the '80s will need a new volume, for they will confront their own unique problems. By then we will also have some idea about what kind of husbands, wives, and parents the present young generation will have become. Doubtless they will succeed in some areas where we have failed. Let us pray that they will not fail where we have succeeded.

QUESTIONS FOR FAMILY
AND GROUP DISCUSSION

[Chapter 1.] What changes do you anticipate taking place in your family in the '70s? What values do you want to guide your family in this decade? What problems do you see emerging from the convergence of male-female roles? What values do you see? What do you perceive as being your most basic needs as a family at the present? Do you agree with Ernest Havemann that an orgasm is more important to a man than to a woman? Why do you think Margaret Mead's proposal about a two-stage marriage would or would not work? If the "trinity of terrors" (conception, infection, detection) are not the real reasons for premarital chastity, what are the real reasons?

[Chapter 2.] Should a couple be completely open and frank with each other about everything? What advantages and/or disadvantages can you see in this practice? What might a couple do where one is the "talk it out" type and the other tends to be a "let's forget it" type? Do you and your mate have a more open relationship now than when you were first married? Why? If you were to rate communication in your marriage on a 1 to 5 scale (with 1 being the best), what score would you give yourself? your mate? What one thing could your mate do to help marital communication? (You might consider sharing answers.) What three things might you do to minimize the "dangers" of honest communication with each other?

[Chapter 3.] Do you agree that all marriages experience conflicts? Can some couples become so well adjusted to each other that they no longer quarrel? Do young couples quarrel more than couples who have been married several years? Is it easier to express genuine love or anger? Do you and your mate quarrel more or less than when you were first married? Why? What is a better way of handling anger than "Kick the Dog," "Bean Pot," etc.? Are you aware of your mate's "beltline"? Does your mate know yours? How can you tell when you have truly forgiven another?

[Chapter 4.] How can we know whether our money possesses us or we possess our money? What should be taken into consideration in deciding who should handle the family money? What is the main money problem that you and your family have? What causes a person to have immature and unrealistic ideas about money? What can be done about this? In looking back over the eight different attitudes that people have toward money as cited in this chapter, which one do you see as being most like yourself? What guidelines should a modern couple follow in the wise use of credit cards? What ways can a person fight back against high-pressure sales gimmicks that lead us to want what we cannot afford, or to buy what we do not need? Do you and your family have fewer money problems now than when you were first married? Why?

[Chapter 5.] Do modern families have more or less time together than their grandparents? Why? What is the main reason why you and your family do not have more time together? Do you feel a need for more or less time now than early in marriage? Has the amount of family time changed with the passing of the years? Why? Respond to this statement: Families do not spend more time together because they really do not enjoy each other that much. Do wives you know have trouble understanding their husbands' work schedules? Do husbands you know have trouble understanding their wives' need for time together? Think of three ways in which more quality could be put into your family time. Think of three corners of "ungleaned" time that your family might use. If you and your mate had a whole day together, how would you like to spend the time?

[Chapter 6.] Do you agree with the statement that all marriages are susceptible to the dry rot? Why? What steps might you take if you feel that dry rot is invading your marriage? What role do good friends play in keeping your marriage alive? Does it mean that a couple has the dry rot if they enjoy having dinner with another couple? What should one do if he finds himself interested in being with a person of the opposite sex other than his mate? Do you think man is basically polygamous or monogamous? What are some unrealistic marital expectations that you think couples have? Respond to this statement: Looks are more important to men than to women. What should a couple do when one has strong needs for demonstrations of love and the mate is very reserved about such matters? What can a person do to develop a healthier sense of self-esteem? Respond to this statement: As persons get older, they have less and less need for touching and for showing love.

[Chapter 7.] If you had to choose, would you rather be a good parent or a good mate? Why? If you were to rate yourself as a parent on a 1 to 5 scale (with 1 being best), what score would you give yourself? Are you doing a better job of being a parent than your parents did? Why? What is the main difference of opinion that you and your mate had regarding your children? Are you stricter or more permissive with your children than your parents were with you? What adjustmental problems did the birth of your children bring into the home? What role should the grandparents play in the rearing of their grandchildren? If you were to try to rank the relative influence of the factors that mold a child's personality, what would be the top five? Respond to this statement: Children should not get married until they can fully support themselves. What is the main joy you derive from being a parent? What do you like least about being a parent?

[Chapter 8.] Do you think the present generation gap is different from past ones? Why? Discuss this statement: The main problem with young people today is that they have had it too easy. Since many of the older generation are proud of how they "came up the hard way," what do you suppose those of the affluent new generation will take pride in? What lessons might the younger generation learn by listening to the older generation? What lessons might the older generation learn from the new generation? What national and world conditions have given rise to the current problems with young people? Why is it that every major nation from Japan to Egypt to Germany has had problems with student unrest?

BIBLIOGRAPHY

Abrahamsen, David, *The Road to Emotional Maturity.* Prentice-Hall, Inc., 1958.

Albrook, Robert, "One Thing Sure, Parenthood Today Is No Bore," *Fortune,* January, 1969, pp. 92–93 ff.

Bach, George, and Wyden, Peter, *The Intimate Enemy.* William Morrow and Company, Inc., 1969.

Beckwith, Burnham, *The Next 500 Years.* The Exposition Press, Inc., 1968.

Bergler, Edmund, *Money and Emotional Conflicts.* Pageant Book Company, 1959.

Berne, Eric, *Games People Play.* Grove Press, Inc., 1964.

Bettelheim, Bruno, *Love Is Not Enough.* The Free Press, 1950.

Blood, Robert, and Wolfe, Donald, *Husbands and Wives: The Dynamics of Married Living.* The Free Press, 1960.

Burenstam Linder, Staffan, *The Harried Leisure Class.* Columbia University Press, 1970.

Burgess, Ernest; Locke, Harvey; and Thomes, Mary, "The Companionate Family," in Hyman Rodman (ed.), *Marriage, Family and Society: A Reader.* Random House, Inc., 1965.

Caldwell, Taylor, *The Listener*. Doubleday & Company, Inc., 1960.

Campbell, Ernest, *Christian Manifesto*. Harper & Row Publishers, Inc., 1970.

Cuber, John, and Harroff, Peggy, *The Significant Americans*. Appleton-Century-Crofts, Inc., 1965.

Denton, Wallace, *The Role of the Minister's Wife*. The Westminster Press, 1962.

——— *What's Happening to Our Families?* The Westminster Press, 1964.

Drucker, Peter, *The Age of Discontinuity*. Harper & Row, Publishers, Inc., 1969.

Duvall, Evelyn, *When You Marry*. Association Press, 1962.

Farson, Richard, *et al., The Future of the Family*. Family Service Association of America, 1969.

Feldman, Harold, and Rollins, Boyd, "Marital Satisfaction Over the Family Life Cycle," *Journal of Marriage and the Family,* February, 1970, pp. 20–28.

Goodman, Paul, "Today's Youth," *Chicago Tribune,* September 14, 1969.

Hunt, Morton, *The Natural History of Love*. Alfred A. Knopf, Inc., 1959.

Keniston, Kenneth, "Stranded in the Present," in Sheldon Garber (ed.), *Adolescence for Adults*. Blue Cross Association, 1969.

Knight, James, *For the Love of Money*. J. B. Lippincott Company, 1968.

LeMasters, E. E., *Parents in Modern America*. The Dorsey Press, Inc., 1970.

Lerner, Max, *America as a Civilization*. Simon and Schuster, Inc., 1957.

Mace, David, "The Art of Marital Fighting," *McCall's,* October, 1962, pp. 50 ff.

McLuhan, Marshall, *Understanding Media.* McGraw-Hill Book Company, Inc., 1964.

Maxey David, "Mr. President, Bring Us Together Again," *Look,* January 27, 1970, pp. 15–18.

Mead, Margaret, "Apprenticeship for Marriage: A Startling Proposal," *Redbook,* October, 1963, pp. 14, 16.

—— and Wolfenstein, Martha (eds.), *Childhood in Contemporary Cultures.* The University of Chicago Press, 1955.

—— *Culture and Commitment: A Study of the Generation Gap.* Doubleday & Company, Inc. / Natural History Press, 1970.

Morrison, Eleanor, "Family Peace at Any Price?" *International Journal of Religious Education,* May, 1967, pp. 8–9 ff.

Ogburn, W. F., and Nimkoff, M. F., *Technology and the Changing Family.* Houghton Mifflin Company, 1955.

Packard, Vance, *The Hidden Persuaders.* David McKay Company, Inc., 1957.

Parsons, Talcott, and Bales, Robert, *Family, Socialization and Interaction Process.* The Free Press, 1955.

Pineo, Peter, "Disenchantment in the Later Years of Marriage," *Marriage and Family Living,* February, 1961, pp. 3–11.

Riesman, David; Denney, Reuel; and Glazer, Nathan, *The Lonely Crowd.* Yale University Press, 1950.

Roszak, Theodore, *The Making of a Counter Culture.* Doubleday & Company, Inc., 1969.

Rymph, Raymond, "Faculty Interview," *Purdue Exponent,* May 22, 1970.

Scanzioni, John, "The Newsletter of Marriage," *Ladies' Home Journal,* December, 1968, p. 22.

Seligman, Daniel, "A Special Kind of Rebellion," *Fortune,* January, 1969, pp. 66–69 ff.

Slater, P. E., "Cultures in Collision," *Psychology Today,* July, 1970, pp. 31–32 ff.

Sugarman, D. A., "How to Cool Your Anger," *Seventeen,* April, 1967, pp. 144 ff.

Tapp, Roland, "Product Analysis and Planning." Unpublished report to Charles Colman III, General Manager, The Westminster Press, 1969.

Udry, Richard, *The Social Context of Marriage.* J. B. Lippincott Company, 1966.

Waller, Willard, *The Family: A Dynamic Interpretation.* The Cordon Co., Inc., 1938.

Winter, Gibson, *Love and Conflict: New Patterns in Family Life.* Doubleday & Company, Inc., 1958.